Sealed, not Healed

Sealed, not Healed

Pregnant in a Pandemic

Gold & Light Publishing House
Cait MacDonell

This book is dedicated to my husband, Rafe.
Thank you for watching our son every Saturday
morning as I wrote. For loving me and us through this
journey. I couldn't have done it without your support.

Also - to the moms who have ever felt alone.
To the moms who have felt distant from God.
To the moms who have walked beside me.
To the moms who have gone before me.
To my mom, sister, and grandma.

You are loved and helped shape
this book into what it is.

Praise for *Sealed, not Healed*

———

"Caitlyn writes with an authenticity and vulnerability that draw you in not only to her personal story, but also to the story that so many of us women face—the story of new life, uncertainty, hope, and the deep change that inevitably accompanies motherhood in all of its beauty. Prepare to be captivated as you turn each page to discover the meaning behind 'Sealed, Not Healed.'"

— Keirsten Jones, Author of "Design Your life"

"A book filled with such beautiful words covering love, sacrifice, and loss. Cait's story truly can meet you where you're at in life. She touches you so deeply through her vulnerability and desire to be like Jesus."

— Alysha Ahrens, fellow mom

"'Sealed, Not Healed' is such an easy book to read—I didn't want to put it down, so much so that I read it in one sitting (thank you, extra-long toddler nap!).
"It was so easy to find solace in Cait's words. Having also gone through pregnancy and childbirth at the same time during the pandemic, a lot of things rang true for me."

— Beckie Paddon, fellow mom

"This book is such an encouragement for hopeful or expecting mamas—really, any mama. Her writing feels like a friend chatting over coffee—you will laugh, and you will feel the comfort of not going through hard things alone. Reading Cait's story will remind you of God's faithfulness and provision, and give you hope for how he will show up in your own story."

— Morgan Roskam, fellow mom

"I was so intrigued—I just had to keep reading... Young women who are expecting or are thinking about it will surely find comfort in learning about some of the trials of motherhood in a way that is reassuring and even helpful."

— Beth Sterling, fellow mom

"Caitlyn's transparency and vulnerability allowed me to see myself through her words. The more I read, the more I was able to reminisce on my own past pregnancies & postpartum experiences. Read this if you want to be reminded that you're not alone in motherhood."

— Esperanza Camara, fellow mom

"As a relatively new mom, I resonated with many of the personal stories Caitlyn shared; I laughed and enjoyed the snippets of good, practical advice! Excited to share this new book with my mom friends!"

— Rachel Nagel, fellow mom

"Becoming a mother can be a lonely journey. Cait demonstrates resilience, strength, and fierce hope amid the hardship of her postpartum story."

— Emily Hartley, fellow mom

"Becoming closer to God through the motherhood journey—an inspiring story that speaks to mothers' strengths. Cait has taught me how to gently embrace challenges of motherhood without feeling lost, reminding me that I am never alone."

— Maddalena Crackett, fellow mom

"The resounding words I hear when I read Cait's book are 'you're not alone.' Cait paints such a captivating picture of what being pregnant is like. No matter what your pregnancy journey has looked like, this book is for you."

— Bethany Small, fellow mom

"Some people are extra good at painting a picture in our minds through their words, and Cait no doubt is one of them. She makes you feel as if you're there with her during these experiences she shares about so openly and deeply.
"This is not your typical '5 teps to a Better Life' book. It feels more like a conversation with a friend, a sweet embrace in regard to who we are as moms and what we go through, a loving reminder of how God is everything we need—not just the assets and gifts He can give us, but simply Himself—the One who sealed us with His love.
"This book is a must-read if you're a new mom, a mom-to-be, or just overall feeling alone or misunderstood in motherhood. 10/10, would recommend."

— Diana Bigby, fellow mom

TABLE OF CONTENTS

———

PREFACE

I primarily wrote *Sealed, not Healed* because God told me to. On the days I didn't want to, I pushed forward, knowing that if God wanted me to do this, He'd help me. I'm also writing this to you because maybe my story can make you feel like you're not alone, that someone else gets it. Because you might be looking for healing too.

I don't think we'll ever be fully healed this side of glory, not until there's no longer any sin in the world or we're in Heaven. But we are sealed because Jesus died for us. He reconciled us to God. He bore the weight of our sin and shame so we could experience forgiveness. But wouldn't it be nice if we could live without pain? I think we're in constant need of healing. We all carry a need to be healed from our pasts and present.

During my pregnancy, I needed God to heal me from the comments people said to me. I needed healing from the trauma of COVID and how it's impacted motherhood for me and my family. I needed healing for my wounds. In the present, I'll always need forgiveness for my lack of patience and the days I neglect to communicate with God. I still need healing for how to love my new body. I need healing as I mourn our old lifestyle (pre-child).

This book is for all the new moms out there that have so much thrown their way. The fear of birth and the opinions of friends, family, strangers, or Western society can make us feel overwhelmed. It's the raw truth of what I went through, and I hope no woman feels alone. Now, looking back, I can see God in each beautiful and challenging moment, and I hope I can show you that He's there for you too.

We don't just need healing; we need the One who heals us, the One who's always with us—Jesus. It's a daily choice to live in that space and to hand our worries, fears, and pain over to Him. Wherever you're at, know you're sealed. Know you're not alone. There's a heavenly Father who loves you. Who will give you strength and everything else you need. You can be healed. Faith can heal you, and all you have to do is believe in the One who died for you.

Sincerely,
Cait

INTRODUCTION

Hi! It's me, Cait, and I'm excited to tell you about this wild journey of pregnancy and birth. A rollercoaster ride that provided me with no indication of what was coming around each corner.

The first thing to note: I wrote my story through my own eyes and experiences and I trekked this journey with my husband. I realize that is not the case with some moms. Please know, when I refer to "husbands," your story may include a "partner" or you may be journeying through motherhood as a single or widowed woman. All of it is okay. This book is inclusive to whatever your current circumstances are. The things to note are our commonalities.

So many of us have this romantic idea when we're little girls—and all the way up to dating or getting married—about what it's like to have a baby. We talk about how many kids we want, where we'd like to live with our precious family, and what it might be like to have a boy versus a girl.

It's funny; now looking back on those daydreams, I realize I had no idea I would have *zero control* of *any* outcome. I mean, it's pretty obvious with the "having a boy or girl" question. You can't necessarily choose that. Unless you're using advanced fertility options, you can't choose exactly when you get pregnant either. But I did think we'd be able to choose where we lived. I didn't imagine that question being a curveball hurtling toward *home* plate, but here we are. I'm writing this to you from my living room in Edinburgh, Scotland. How did I get here? Well, I'm still wrapping my mind around that, but let's start at the beginning . . .

CHAPTER ONE

You're Glowing! No, That's Sweat

FINDING OUT WE WERE PREGNANT

———

Rafe and I married on January 4, 2020, in Portland, Oregon, which is where I grew up. At the time, we were living in London, England, which was the middle point between our homes. Rafe is from Zimbabwe. We had family from all over the world fly in to celebrate our love and how God brought us together. Despite the number of guests who traveled there, we planned to have two more weddings that year. Yes, two. I know that sounds like a bit much, but we wanted to celebrate with all of the people who had loved us so well up to that point in our lives. The plan was to have a London wedding at our church that summer and a "Zim" wedding in December.

I couldn't wait for my family to see the continent I had fallen in love with over the years. I knew Africa well by that point. I had spent time in Uganda, Tanzania, South Africa, and Zimbabwe. But we all know what happened that year, don't we? The virus that need not be named—okay, COVID-19—caused a global pandemic.

We couldn't complain about not getting to have two more weddings; it was a blessing to have had even one that year. I tell people now that it was the last party of the year since so many of our friends who were planning to get married then had to postpone their weddings or deal with the ever-changing restrictions.

Before Rafe and I were married, I moved into our one-bedroom flat off of Golborne Road, right next to Portobello Road in Notting Hill. If you are unsure where that is, then I'll help you out. It is by the market in the opening scene of the movie we all love, Notting Hill. Yep. "I'm just a girl, standing in front of a boy, asking him to love her." We chose that location because I worked for the local parish church, St. Peter's. It was the ideal place to live—so close to our church community—and I absolutely loved walking through the market to work.

Sadly, walking to work came to a halt on March 16, 2020, when London entered its first lockdown. The first thing we noticed was that we lived next to a fire station. It often sounded like all of London was on fire with the number of sirens we heard throughout the day.

With everything closed around us and the fear of the pandemic, could anything else possibly surprise us? In short, yes.

———

I'm not sure about you or where you're at in your life journey, but I feared that I wouldn't be able to fall pregnant. I don't know where that fear came from. It could have been from the movies I'd watched or because women are now more openly talking about their struggles with infertility.

Don't get me wrong; I believe awareness of the difficulties is important to normalize, especially since it seems that right after you get married there comes the question: "So when are you having babies?" It's pressure that doesn't help anyone. I mean, I get it . . . I've likely asked someone this question before, but I saved it for dear friends, not a group or public setting. Having a baby is a personal choice, and it's a decision of not only *when*, but also *if*.

The enemy, as part of his *modus operandi*, will try to plant seeds of fear or doubt into the minds of God-loving people. He did it to me before Rafe and I had even tried to get pregnant. It was a little whisper in my ear, saying, "Do you think you can even have kids? You probably can't." Then I ruminated on all of the possibilities of how we wouldn't be able to conceive.

Then I jumped ahead further. So would we foster?

Adopt? Would we keep trying? Would we consider in-vi-tro fertilization (IVF)? Could we even afford to try that?

The "what if" game can be a dangerous one. I became lost in the terrible imagery, not focusing on our current reality. We'd only been married a little over two months, and I was already wrestling with these intense thoughts. I even asked people to pray for us—pray that we'd be able to have kids. A wise older couple in our church gently reminded us (mainly me): "It's only been two months; enjoy your first year of marriage."

Taking deep breaths would calm me down, and I'd think, *Okay, well, it's probably going to take us a while anyway, and if we can't, God will guide us on what to do next.*

On March 18, two days after lockdown, I realized "shark week"—yes, I call my period *shark week*—was late. I casually decided to take a pregnancy test, leaving it on the bathroom floor and heading back to the living room to watch whatever we were bingeing on TV before looking at the results.

A few minutes later, Rafe headed into the bathroom. He looked down and saw the pregnancy test. Yelling into the living room, just as casually as I had left the test, he let me know that I wasn't pregnant.

Well of course not. I didn't think I would be. I zoned back into the show we were watching. Less than a minute later, I heard, "Cait . . . Caaaait! Come in here." I strode to the bathroom, wondering what happened.

Once I reached the threshold, I looked at him, and he at me. Then, we both looked down at the test—the one that now read *pregnant*. We just stared at each other. We didn't cry like I thought I would. Instead, it felt like we were the actors in a slow-motion movie scene where the music has stopped, and everyone is left thinking, "Wait, what?"

After a minute of staring, which felt like an hour (we're dramatic), we laughed and hugged one another. Then, my heart deflated a bit. "Wait a minute! You found out before me!"

I had always thought I would come up with some creative way to tell Rafe we were pregnant if it ever did happen. I don't know, something like wrapping up a present and filming him opening it. Okay, maybe not that. We've all seen that a hundred times . . . but something!

"Can you go get two more tests to make sure this is real?" I asked him. Later, we were told that it's a lot harder to get a false positive than a false negative.

The true excitement started to seep in once we confirmed the news two more times over, and I wanted to step outside and shout it to anyone who could hear me. It would only have been our closest neighbors since we were all stuck inside, because, you know . . . COVID. Relief and joy intermingled in my soul, giving me the feeling of utter peace.

The general rule of thumb is to wait twelve weeks before announcing a pregnancy. We found out at the five-week mark, and we told our family that very day. We shared the news with our closest friends in the following few days. We couldn't contain ourselves; we were bubbling over with excitement.

Why do people usually wait? Well, the first twelve weeks of pregnancy contain the highest risk for miscarriage. I learned that one in four women in America miscarries, so it's a very real possibility. The reason we decided not to wait was because if that happened, I wouldn't want to keep it to myself. I'd need the support of my family and friends to help us get through something that difficult. Plus, with everything happening around the world, our pregnancy was just about the only positive news our group of family and friends had.

As much as living abroad is glorified, it also has its challenges—finding a new hairdresser, for example. *Impossible!* For real, I haven't found the right person in three years. Another difficulty of living abroad was that telling our family on video calls was not how I imagined it would go down. I envisioned hugging and dancing. But even without the lockdown, it probably would have been on video for most of our friends and family since I'm terrible at keeping a secret. What was so hard was that we didn't have the option to tell anyone in person.

Pregnant and isolated in a global pandemic, I was put in the high-risk category for getting COVID-19. It was yet another fear to deal with. I could only have a positive mindset for so many days in a row; then, I would just burst into tears, permitting myself to cry.

I'd read on multiple forums that when you're pregnant and in an anxious, stressed, or fearful state, the stress hormones released into your bloodstream then cross through the placenta to the baby. This caused varying alarm bells to ring in my mind. I didn't want to cause my baby any stress, and that fear only added to my own stress! I had to learn how to manage all my twisting emotions, which was hard since my hormones were changing as well. I knew bottling things up wasn't going to work. Whenever I felt sad about my circumstances, I reminded myself of what sadness meant. This emotion flags the loss of something we value. So instead of focusing on what I'd lost—in-person celebrations, a safe environment, and so on—I focused on those I loved. This focus was a reminder of the love I have for my family and friends and the desire to be with them.

A lot of things felt taken away from me throughout my early pregnancy, but as I'd soon learn, it was only the beginning. Once I knew I was pregnant, so did my phone. Some unknown AI program started recommending videos of the different ways people tell their loved ones about the big news (in person, of course). My tears fell as I watched, all of them reminders of my isolation.

If you're deciding how to share news of your pregnancy with loved ones, I don't advise watching those videos. Well, not as many as I did—unless you need some inspiration. Why? Because every person and every family are different. The videos built up an expectation of how people would (should?) respond to my news. When my loved ones didn't respond with tears—even though I hadn't either—or weren't screaming and dancing with joy, I was hurt. It sounds absolutely ridiculous, but I was already beginning to fall into the comparison game. I didn't realize it would start so early in pregnancy. That's the worst thing about social media now; we compare every little detail of our lives, details we may not have even considered comparing before. At least, I did. So I put my phone down and took a long break. Then, I downloaded Mario Kart, which I spent an insane amount of time playing.

———

At around seven weeks, I thought, "Wow! Maybe I'll be one of those women who don't have morning sickness!" Ha. I can't even believe I thought that. By the way, if you are one of those women who didn't get morning sickness, don't tell other pregnant women. That's just not nice.

So here comes the morning . . . well, for me, *night*

sickness. It was always 7:30 p.m., on the dot, when I would start to throw up. The nausea was intense. I even tried the nasty ginger candies everyone recommended, but nothing seemed to help. And I would get a metallic taste in my mouth, which made my tongue feel weird. I grew extremely tired, so it was basically throw up, then pass out. Now that I think about it, it sounds like a night out gone wrong. The funny thing was that I took some maternity photos of myself during this time. I later realized, *Yes, my baby was in there*, but in reality I had simply documented my bloated stomach. Bloated and beautiful, I tell you. Bloated and beautiful!

Then came my nose. With its super sensitivity, I thought, *This is how dogs must smell!* I could smell anything from any distance, and it all smelled horrible. When I ventured out for my permitted daily exercise, I could only make it a few blocks before having to retire back to home base. I couldn't handle the smells around me. Thankfully, I only threw up once on the side of the road—not a fun thing to do in general, but especially when you're living in a pandemic. I felt like I had the plague as people walked to the other side of the street or turned around to avoid me. I can't blame them; I'd probably have done the same.

I felt fortunate that I was able to work from home. I couldn't imagine having to be in the workplace around others as they ate their lunches or having to use a shared bathroom. Home quarantine was difficult, but it was also one of the few positives about this whole season.

Then came the question pregnant women get asked countless times: "So . . . what are you craving? Anything weird?" I wish I was asked about how I was feeling. How is pregnancy going so far? Nope.

My answer made people's eyebrows pinch together. "Just chugging milk, which I never have before, and eating potatoes and fruit."

I felt like a little girl again. I wanted the comfort food my mom made me when I was little, things like vegetable soup. You know, nostalgic food. Food often brings back the memories of times when I was cared for. My answer was not what people wanted to hear. They wanted to hear that I craved pickles dipped in chocolate or some other crazy food combination. Since I didn't say that, I felt as if I had disappointed them. Their confused faces told me I had let them down because I didn't have some weird craving.

On the other hand, the smell or even the thought of meat would make me want to gag. *This is it! I'll never eat bacon again!* A tragic assumption, I know. Meanwhile, Rafe was trying to get me to eat veggies, not just starches. I knew he didn't understand what I was going through. But it was almost as if he didn't believe me when I complained about the nausea. "I don't want to eat carrots!" I remember telling him a hundred times. For some odd reason, he kept insisting on them.

Thankfully, we both have older sisters who had

been pregnant before me. I would often say to Rafe, "Go call your sister, Ayshah." And she'd help him understand.

> *Side note to pregnant women: My suggestion to you, if you're pregnant—or become pregnant one day—is to connect with a woman who's gone before you so she can explain things to your husband. Trust me.*

A piece of advice that really helped me in this trimester—as if you're not getting enough advice already—is something my sister, Sarah, told me. One day, I was in tears. I kept thinking, *Why did I want to have a baby? This is so hard!* Then, *That's it! I'm only going to have one child!* I didn't think I could ever do this again—the isolation, the cravings, the sickness. My sister told me, "It's your first. That's why it's so hard. You don't know the love you will feel when you meet your baby. Just wait. Everything you are going through will be worth it!" In the end, she couldn't have been more correct. This pregnancy-hormone-craziness, food-aversion-night-sickness season was all new to me, and some days, it was easier to think that maybe I didn't want to be pregnant. Afterward, the guilt of even thinking that haunted me. I had to battle against my invasive thoughts and lean on my sister's words: *This will be worth it.*

So there we were, in lockdown. We'd told the family our news, my body felt like crap, and then surprise! Rafe gets put on furlough. The furlough scheme made it so Rafe would get paid only 70 percent of his salary from the government while not being able to work. Since this was the beginning of the COVID pandemic, no one knew how long the furlough would last. We decided we were going to view it as a blessing.

Rafe was an absolute champion at taking care of me the way he did—cooking for us and making me a daily morning smoothie. It didn't take me long to figure out it was because that was the only way to get me to eat my veggies. The best part—well, not the best, but it's in the top three—was he did all of the grocery shopping. The man would be gone for hours! I understood there was a queue outside, and everyone had to walk a certain way throughout the grocery store, but to be gone for hours? How was that possible? I'd never been at the food store that long and never wanted to be. It turned out Rafe was comparing everything. Prices. Ingredients. You name it. I'm pretty sure he knew every deal and learned the location of every item in the store. I'm surprised they didn't try to hire him. It's funny looking back at that time. He even inventoried every item we owned in some app on his phone. Sometimes that drove me crazy, but it gave him something to do. The man had nothing but time on his hands, and he used it to take care of us. I'm so thankful that he was there for me and could deal with my ever-changing emotions.

The next thing that was taken away from me by this virus was Rafe not being able to be with me for our first ultrasound appointment. It was devastating to say the least.

We had our 12 week appointment at St. Mary's Hospital, the place where The Royals are born. I mean, I totally knew I was going to have a little prince! In truth, we were only there because St. Mary's was the closest hospital to our house, and trust me, we were not getting the royal treatment. We ended up renting a local car share since I didn't feel comfortable taking public transportation. We found a place to park, then Rafe helped me find the correct building, gave me a hug, and left me with the words, "I'll be right here."

Mask on, I made my way into the hospital. I sat in the waiting room with other pregnant women, honoring space by staying a few seats apart. When a new woman would arrive, the lady at the desk would tell her partner he couldn't be there. You could feel the sadness in the room, the collective desire not to be alone. *At least we're all in this together*, I thought.

Eventually, my name got called, and I headed into the ultrasound room. I wasn't sure how I was going to react, seeing our baby for the first time. I didn't know if I was going to cry or squeal or lie there in awe-filled silence. Honestly, I felt that if I didn't cry, maybe something was wrong with me.

Side note to pregnant women: However you respond to seeing your baby is how you respond; it's not something you control or should feel you have to force. I've learned that I'm not a crier— that's more my husband's style—and that's okay.

Lying down with jelly on my tummy, I looked up at the screen, and there was our beautiful baby. I had a deep sense of knowing, knowing that the baby was *mine*, and I loved him with all of my heart. I didn't want the ultrasound to stop. I just wanted to keep watching him move, to see him wiggling about. I was falling in love with this little human on the screen, and I couldn't wait to meet him. *What will he be like?* I wondered. Would he have my mouth or my nose? Would he have Rafe's curly blond hair? All in all, it wouldn't matter much. I just wanted him to be healthy and happy.

After the appointment was finished, I paid to get a few of the scans printed and headed back to Rafe. The look on his face when he saw our baby was priceless. There was so much love in his eyes. We embraced and headed back to our little flat, nestled together in a joint expression of gratitude. And excited to share the photo with the rest of our family!

New Momma Prayer

Jeremiah 1:5 says, "Before I formed you in the womb I knew you, before you were born I set you apart."

God, I thank you for the miracle of life. I thank you for knowing my baby. Lord, you know my every need. Be my strength in the moments I feel weak. Nourish my body to sustain me in this pregnancy. May you have the glory as I surrender this body to you. No matter what symptoms may come my way, I praise you. You created my body to bring life into this world. Help me love each moment. Hold me close and catch my tears when I feel overwhelmed. With you, I can do all things. Remind me, Lord. I say this to you as your daughter. As your little girl. As this baby grows inside of me, may I continue to grow more in love and be dependent on you. In Jesus's name, Amen.

CHAPTER TWO

Mary, Did You Know?

LEARNING FROM MARY'S PREGNANCY

——

You may have heard the song *Mary, Did You Know?* originally by Mark Lowry. If you haven't, pause and have a quick listen, paying special attention to the first line, and then note my changes:

"Caitlyn, did you know
that your baby boy
would one day pee on your face?"

The remaining verses in the lyrics are questions to Mary about her expectations and experiences as the mother of Jesus.

Becoming pregnant and dealing with questions can

be overwhelming—or just plain annoying.

- Were you trying to get pregnant?
- Do you have a name picked out?
- You're going to breastfeed, right?
- Are you going to get an epidural or have a natural birth?

Our questions aren't as intense as Mary's. After all, she was carrying the Son of God. But still, the weight of the invasive inquiries can crush your joy. Nonetheless, Mary said yes to all of that. She said yes to questions that seemed impossible to answer and when she knew she would be judged by so many people. It's not like people were asking her the above questions at the time, but she *did* say yes to giving birth to the Son of God. I think that's the biggest question she could have possibly said yes to. Let's dive into the Scripture below and see how Mary found out she was going to become pregnant, what she asked, and how she responded:

Luke 1:30–38: The Birth of Jesus Foretold

In the sixth month of Elizabeth's pregnancy, God sent the angel Gabriel to Nazareth, a town in Galilee, to a virgin pledged to be married to a man named Joseph, a descendant of David. The virgin's name was Mary. The angel went to her and said, "Greetings, you who are highly favored! The Lord is with you."

Mary was greatly troubled at his words and wondered what kind of greeting this might be. But the angel said to her, "Do not be afraid, Mary; you have found favor with God. You will conceive and give birth to a son, and you are to call him Jesus. He will be great and will be called the Son of the Most High. The Lord God will give him the throne of his father David, and he will reign over Jacob's descendants forever; his kingdom will never end."

"How will this be," Mary asked the angel, "since I am a virgin?"

The angel answered, "The Holy Spirit will come on you, and the power of the Most High will overshadow you. So the holy one to be born will be called the Son of God. Even Elizabeth your relative is going to have a child in her old age, and she who was said to be unable to conceive is in her sixth month. For no word from God will ever fail."

"I am the Lord's servant," Mary answered. "May your word to me be fulfilled." Then the angel left her.

Today, we find out we're pregnant when we pee on a stick and two lines, a plus sign, or the word *positive* emerge. Mary, on the other hand, found out from an angel. I'm pretty sure I would be startled and afraid if an angel came to visit me and told me I would be carrying the Messiah. And it seems that she felt that way too. She was troubled, and the angel could see it in her expression and told her not to be afraid. "You are favored."

If you are afraid, I just want to stop and say that God is with you. Maybe an angel hasn't come to visit you, but you're not alone. It's okay to feel afraid. I'll say it again: trust that God is with you, and he'll bring people around you to help you in this season.

The angel then tells Mary she's going to give birth to God's son! Casual, right? And not only that, but this son is going to rule over all and his kingdom will never end. (At least she didn't have to pick out a name like we do!) The angel basically answered the questions presented in *Mary Did You Know?*—just not in great detail. That's what surprises me. Mary doesn't ask much. She never doubts by asking, "Well, how is He going to rule? When is He going to rule? What next steps do I need to take? Why will people follow Him? Do you have a curriculum for me to teach Him on how to rule? Are there some videos I can watch on how to raise or discipline my Son? Does He need special sensory toys?" She doesn't ask anything like that. The only thing she wants to know is *how it will happen*. She's a virgin, and I think this is a valid question. Yet she doesn't obsess about the details like we do today. She hears a word from God and trusts it. Period.

If you're in your first trimester, are you trusting everything will be okay? If you're still trying for a baby, do you trust that God has put that desire in your heart for a reason?

It's hard not to google a million things before, during, and after pregnancy. To want to figure out every detail about what's happening to your body and how your baby is growing. It is easy to google first and pray later. I get it: you have questions, and it is wise to learn about what you're going through and how your body is changing or will change. But please remember that prayer and God's promises trump worldly information.

How amazing is it that Mary questioned God, too, by asking the angel, "How is this going to happen?" Especially since it seemed downright impossible. The angel lets Mary know the Holy Spirit will come upon her and overshadow (i.e., impregnate) her. I mean, duh— why didn't she think of that? Even though that sounds absolutely impossible, Mary replies, "May your word to me be fulfilled." She doesn't say, "Well, I hope this works out," and then doubt the promise. She has full confidence and faith in God. My hope for you is that you have full confidence that God is going to see you through your desires and your pregnancy, no matter what happens.

One of my favorite parts of this full passage above is that the angel tells her she isn't in this alone. Her relative, Elizabeth, is also pregnant—miraculously pregnant since she's so old—and everyone in her community is in awe. I love that we never have to journey alone. That's the beauty of Christianity and motherhood. There are family members, friends, or other moms who have been pregnant or are pregnant at the same time, ready to support you. God often brings specific people into your life at just the right time. Mary didn't just have a relative who was pregnant; she had a relative who had received a miracle—just like her. There's something special in knowing that you're not the only one going through something.

How encouraging that so many women have gone before us? That so many can relate to what we're going through? Knowing that I wasn't the first person to ever give birth brought me comfort. I pulled strength from the women who had gone before me, including the women in the Bible. I read and reread this passage and asked God, "What are you teaching us about You? How can Mary's story encourage me? What does this show all of us about pregnancy?"

1. Communion with God.

Pregnancy, giving birth, and being a mom can be hard, and that's okay. God wants to hear all about it. I found myself praying the most in the bathtub. I'd light a few candles, drop in some lavender, listen to a peaceful piano playlist, and rest my head on my bathtub pillow.

Side note: If you don't have a bathtub pillow, get one.

It was a space where my mind could relax and where my body was most at ease. It's where I talked to God about my day, how I was feeling, the questions I had, and where I expressed gratitude to Him. I thanked Him for all He was doing and was going to do in my life. I thanked Him for answering my prayer about becoming a mom. I thanked Him for knowing His plans for my life and going before me. I thanked Him that I don't need to be afraid because He is always with me. I practiced gratitude because it helped get my mind into a positive place.

When you practice having a thankful mindset, everything about your circumstance starts to change. You focus on what is good around you, not what's hard. If I just focused on my nausea or exhaustion, what good would that have done me?

My time with God was also a time when I questioned him. *Why?* Why do I have more symptoms than other women I know? How am I going to get through this without my family nearby? It's a lockdown, and I'm struggling, God . . . *why?*

I wish I could say an angel floated down onto the toilet seat next to the bathtub and decided to have a chat with me. Nope. Not every question was answered, and I don't think all of them ever will be, at least this side of Heaven. What I do know is that I was heard. Friends near and far sent flowers and people from our church dropped off cake at our door. We were celebrated and God was using people to make me feel loved. I felt significant and surrounded by happiness despite the physical distance. God knew I needed that. He knew I used to buy myself flowers every week and that receiving them would elicit pure joy.

Commune with God. He knows your every need, but He'd love to hear it from you directly. Wait and see how He responds. Keep your eyes open, your mind thankful, and you'll soon see the blessings that surround you.

2. All we have to do is say yes.

Besides eating healthy, exercising, taking prenatal vitamins if prescribed, and resting, there's really nothing you need to do. Let's be real: we don't all eat perfectly healthy during pregnancy, so try not to be too hard on yourself. Caramel was my bestie, and I learned to be okay with that. Some days, a pint of salted caramel ice cream was what I needed. No judgment here.

But now, let's try to let it sink in that we, as women, have the ability to grow a human! God designed our bodies to do so. How incredible is that? It baffles my mind how our hormones and bodies change as our babies grow. It truly is a miracle. I mean, we all know what it takes for them to be made. Whether you were trying to have a baby or not, you do have the choice to say yes. To say yes to having a baby, to being a mom, to putting someone else first, to taking care of your body, to having your finances change in preparation for them arriving—there is a lot to say yes to. A lot of things change when a baby comes into the picture. Probably some yeses you might not even know about yet. We also know there is an opportunity to say no. If we continue to think about Mary's story, she was told the Holy Spirit was going to impregnate her. Later, when she was in her third trimester, she traveled ninety miles to the city of Joseph's ancestors, a journey that took her along the flatlands of the Jordan River and then over the hills surrounding Jerusalem and into Bethlehem. With Joseph by her side, Mary road a donkey to a town where there were no available rooms. I'm pretty sure none of us have "give birth in a stable" in our birth plans. I bet it wasn't in Mary's plan either, but she still said yes.

When we get pregnant, none of us really knows where or how it's going to happen. I never thought I'd get an emergency C-section. But all in all, it didn't matter how or where I gave birth or if it was a part of my plan or not. I had a little life growing inside me, and I knew I'd do everything I could to protect that life. I trusted in God's plan and put my pregnancy and our child's birth in His hands.

Throughout pregnancy, birth, and motherhood, who knows what circumstances are going to come our way. But do know this: no matter what your story is, God will use your yes for His good. He will be there for you through the flatlands and the hillsides.

3. He knows who we need.

Why did the angel mention Elizabeth to Mary? This is how I heard it: "Mary, God is the God of miracles. He is a man of His Word. Your relative is pregnant; you are not alone." Okay, I paraphrased a lot, but that's how it clicked in my head. If you're pregnant, try to meet other pregnant women! Join a Facebook community group. Figure out a way to surround yourself with women walking through the same season of life. That's why Mary went to stay with Elizabeth. They needed each other; we need each other.

I am so thankful that God gave me Sophia, Hannah, Steph, Alexis, Alex, Beckie, and the other amazing ladies from my NCT (National Childbirth Trust) group who were pregnant and had due dates around the same time as me. I had a tribe of women to talk to at all hours of the night, ask questions of, and answer questions for. We laughed about how often we discussed boobs, poop, and gas. My group collectively prayed for our babies and dreamed about what was next. And of course, we need people to go on long walks and find fellowship with. We all desire to be loved and known. And, soon-to-be momma (is that you?), these ladies may not come knocking at your door. It might not be your best friend, especially if she isn't pregnant at the same time as you. You may have to actively look for these confidantes. Start praying for the women you will soon find.

You need them, and I believe God is going to bless you with them. Just like for Mary, God has a sister in Christ in mind, one who will walk alongside you. Amen.

4. God's Word and promises never fail.

The Scripture above ends with "For no word from God will ever fail." Spoiler alert: Everything the angel said to Mary happened. Do you believe God's Word and promises for your life? For your pregnancy? For the birth? To know God's Word you have to . . . well, know God's Word. Instead of ending this chapter with a prayer, I'm ending it with Scripture for you to pray, meditate on, and trust in:

"For I know the plans I have for you," declares the Lord, "plans to prosper you and not to harm you, plans to give you hope and a future." (Jeremiah 29:11)

"Come to me, all you who are weary and burdened, and I will give you rest. Take my yoke upon you and learn from me, for I am gentle and humble in heart, and you will find rest for your souls." (Matthew 11:28–29)

"Peace I leave with you; my peace I give you. I do not give to you as the world gives. Do not let your hearts be troubled and do not be afraid." (John 14:27)

"Give your burdens to the Lord, and he will take care of you." (Psalm 55:22)

"Don't be afraid, for I am with you. Don't be discouraged, for I am your God. I will strengthen you and help you. I will hold you up with my victorious right hand." (Isaiah 41:10)

CHAPTER THREE

Lemon Going On Watermelon

THE JOY AND PAIN OF THE SECOND TRIMESTER

———

Like many women who find out they're pregnant, I downloaded an app or two or . . . let's be real—more like four. Most apps tell you what's happening to your body and the size of your baby week by week. For some reason, everyone compares growing humans to fruit. I'd love to see someone come up with an app comparing our babies to what we're craving. For example, *your baby is now the size of a bagel with cream cheese.*

Anyway, back to fruit. When my baby was the size of a lemon, I thought, "No way! It looks like there's at least a small watermelon in there." After all, the size of my growing belly told me so.

Many of these apps also tell you that the second

trimester is much better than the first. Because of that promise, I was counting the weeks, days, minutes, and seconds until I could get there. Week 13 came along, and I assumed that magically on that day I would have energy again and the morning (night) sickness would stop. Did that happen? Nope.

It wasn't until Week 16 that I found some measure of relief. It was a reminder that since no body is the same, no pregnancy is either. What also came with Week 16 was feeling my baby kick for the first time. There were fluttering butterflies in my tummy. I was so excited and couldn't even believe the experience was real! It made *everything* feel real. Like, *Wow! There really is a baby in there*. Sadly, Rafe couldn't feel the baby's movement yet, but I was loving every moment of it. The kicks and fluttering had me wondering what this little human would be like. I delighted in each kick and hoped he'd be a soccer player, just like his mom.

Boy or Girl

As we approached Week 18, it was time to find out the baby's gender. I felt shocked by how many people had an opinion about this. It wasn't something I expected. It nearly turned into a tug of war. Some people told us not to find out, and if we did, they told us we'd be ruining the surprise. Others agreed with us and told us to go for it because knowing helps soon-to-be parents plan ahead. It's hard when people give their opinions, especially when you don't ask for them.

I feel like going on a rant about this, but as my dad would tell me, "Your grandma Pat would always say, 'If you have nothing nice to say, then don't say anything at all.'" Maybe people need to learn a new phrase that can apply to others' pregnancies: "If you aren't asked for your opinion, then don't say anything at all." Or, "If you aren't asked for your opinion, then just listen." I think either of those would be great!

Side note: Decide what you want to do regarding knowing the gender ahead of time and stand your ground.

Finding out the gender of our baby was something that both Rafe and I wanted to do. I didn't want to keep calling our baby an "it" or "him/her." And I didn't like it when people called my baby "bump." I wanted to say "my son" or "my daughter." I wanted to bond more deeply with the baby growing in my tummy.

Have you ever gone through *The 5 Love Languages* test? If you haven't, I recommend taking the assessment with your husband. (It can be found online.) It's super helpful on how to best love one another. The five love languages are physical touch, quality time, acts of service, words of affirmation, and receiving gifts. Now, instead of applying this to a relationship, I want to apply it to being pregnant.

No matter what, you'll get quality time and physical touch because the baby is growing inside you. I think about acts of service as the kicks the baby gives me (yes, a bit of a stretch, I suppose). Now, I'm a "words of affirmation" kind of person, so having the words *son, my boy*, or *bubba* meant so much to me. As for gifts, I'd rather pick out my present and then have someone wrap it. But you could be different from me, and perhaps you enjoy being surprised when you open a gift. In your case, maybe waiting *is* for you. There's no wrong or right way to do this, so do what excites you most.

A question I was asked repeatedly was, "Do you want a boy or a girl?" This was a question I didn't mind being asked, but when it was asked every day, it became excessive. I felt guilty for wanting a girl, so I didn't know if I should even tell people. For some reason, I just knew I was having a boy. I wanted a girl because I had grown up with a sister, and that was all I knew. Especially since on my mom's side of the family, I had mainly female cousins.

After a lot of reflection, at the end of the day, I knew I'd be happy with either. I knew that, boy or girl, I'd be outside playing sports with them as they grew up. So if you have a preference right now, that's okay. You don't need to feel guilty about that. Guilt wants to snatch your joy away from you throughout pregnancy and mother-hood. Do your best to not let it and share with others when you feel it creep in.

Since the hospitals were still not allowing anyone

to have their husband with them for an ultrasound, Rafe and I decided to go get one done privately. Off we went to a place called Window to the Womb. When we arrived, we had to sit outside in the rain to fill out the paperwork. Once we were called inside, we were offered various packages to choose from. On one side of the room, there was a wall of shelves filled with stuffed animals. We learned that one of the packages we could choose provided a recording of our baby's heartbeat, which was then placed in a stuffed animal. Since I couldn't pick a package fast enough (so many choices!), we waited until after our scan to decide.

As we left the waiting room and went into a private room, we met our sonographer. Looking at him and hearing his accent, I knew he was Ugandan, which got me super excited. That was where Rafe and I met, where we still had family, and where I had spent a lot of time in ministry and doing photography. I looked at Rafe and could tell he was thinking the same thing, so he asked the sonographer if he was Ugandan.

"Yes!"

Rafe started speaking to him in Luganda. "*Oli otya ssebo.*"

And you should have seen the joy on this man's face! He told the lady next to him, "That's my language!" It was a beautiful moment, and I could feel God's sweet presence in the room. For the rest of the ultrasound, we were laughing and talking about Uganda. Then, it was time to see if we were having a boy or a girl. He asked us if we wanted to know.

"Yes, but not today." I looked away, and I asked Rafe to do the same.

Well, Rafe "accidentally" (so he says) saw the images on the screen and shouted, "It's a boy!" So that was how we found out. Rafe discovered I was pregnant before me, and he knew the gender of our baby before me!

As we were leaving, I said goodbye in Luganda, and the sonographer looked shocked. "No way! You speak the language too?" I let him know I spoke more of it than Rafe. We opened the door—all laughing together and speaking in Luganda, and the couple in the waiting room looked at us wondering what was happening. It was the joy of the Lord—the joy of finding out we were having a son and having a piece of our story include meeting a new friend from Uganda. I love that God knows exactly how to surprise us and bring us joy. He knew it had been a hard time for us with sickness, isolation, and more, but he sent reminders to us, pointing us to the truth that He was with us. He was (and still is!) for us. He loves making his children feel known.

As we checked out from our appointment, you better believe I decided to pick out a stuffed animal. After hearing our baby's heartbeat, I wanted to hear it over and over. I already cherished that little life inside me. The stuffed animal we chose was a mammoth. I cuddled it for weeks. In the end, not being able to see my family, I decided to mail it as a surprise to my mom. She was able to show it to my niece and nephew. It made the process feel special, that they could be a part of my pregnancy, hearing my little boy's heartbeat, even from afar.

Blue or Pink

Next up was the gender reveal! We couldn't do a big in-person reveal with many people there, so we headed to the English countryside to film a reveal with my sister-in-law and her family. It worked out perfectly because their back garden had a soccer goal. We bought a tiny soccer ball that we filled with blue powder. Rafe was going to toss it at me, and I would kick it, causing the powder to explode out and reveal that we were having a boy!

Even though we already knew our baby's gender, it was so much fun to do. After filming, we created a video for our family and friends to watch together on everybody's favorite video platform: Zoom. The sweetest parts were the guesses from our niece and nephews. The best guess of all was Wendell's. He hoped I was having a dinosaur and was devastated (including tears) to find out I wasn't.

Creature Comforts

As I progressed further into my second trimester,

the weather in London had become scorching hot. I'm used to living in Oregon in the USA. When it was hot, I'd go swimming at my dad's pool, boating at my mom's, or floating on the river with friends. There was always a way to cool off, and most homes had air condition-ing. Not the case in London. There were pools—or in London terms, *lidos*—but there weren't any public lidos open during the pandemic.

Rafe and I decided to bring one into our flat. Yup, we bought a kid's blow-up pool, and I filled it with water. It made for a great Instagram picture, but that was about it. When we returned from one of our walks, we dis-covered our place was not only hotter, but also more humid. The pool was an utter failure. It was back to cold baths, trying to do anything to cool down.

In our flat, we only had two windows, both facing the front, which meant no airflow. It felt like we were trapped. One time, I escaped to a nearby coffee shop and felt I as if I was in Heaven in the air conditioning. Unfortunately, I had arrived at 2:40 p.m., not realizing they were closing at 3:00. I wanted to cry. Honestly, I probably did cry. I was overheating from being preg-nant.

I constantly hid from the sun because I would get so sunburned, and my walk had officially turned into a waddle. With all this, we decided it was time to get out of London and go on a babymoon!

The Babymoon

I learned that from August to the end of September is one of the busiest times for Airbnbs, as it's the summer holiday season. I called as many places as I could. There was absolutely nothing available. I felt desperate to find anywhere to go to get out of our flat. Instead of looking more (since it was driving me mad), I decided to pray, asking God to make a way and find a place for us to stay. Thankfully, within the next few days, he answered that prayer. *Hallelujah!* I was talking to my mentor, Nicole, and she asked one of her friends if her holiday home was available. And indeed, it was!

It was a beautiful home in the English countryside, nestled next to a river with an apple tree out front. It looked like the home from the movie *The Holiday*— the one where Cameron Diaz and Kate Winslet swap homes. The funny thing was, I think the house was built for short people. Rafe had to duck his head to enter any room. He may have even hit his head a few times; it was hard not to laugh in our little hobbit home. We enjoyed sitting in the river to cool off, watching movies, and playing board games in the garden for the week, finally finding some peace in the crazy pandemic heatwave. Nature is good for the soul. It was as if Psalm 23 came to life:

The Lord is my shepherd, I lack nothing.

He makes me lie down in green pastures,

he leads me beside quiet waters,

he refreshes my soul (verses 1–3).

Grief

It was getting harder, though, not seeing my family. There was an inherent unease in knowing that my third trimester was approaching, and even if the whole pandemic turned around, I wouldn't be advised to fly. The journey was not going how I imagined having a baby would go, but I don't think anyone imagined 2020 and how it would impact everything. I tried to focus on the positives. I went for days feeling happy and then, randomly, I'd simply cry over the losses I was experiencing. The loss of not having my niece Addison or nephew Wendell feel my baby kick. Not getting to swim and float in my dad's pool. Being unable to watch movies or have my mom make my favorite meals. I longed to be a little girl again just one last time before I became a mom.

Many times, I bottled up all of my sadness, trying to pretend it didn't exist, and then, out of nowhere, my face would flood with tears. I realized that was not a sustainable way to live . . . and certainly not healthy for my marriage. It was time I truly allowed myself to mourn what COVID had taken away.

I knew I had to talk about what I was feeling. I had to let my husband in and not push him away. For some reason, when I'm upset, I don't like to be touched. Through my pregnancy, that got even worse for me. I didn't want any affection. I even googled for info, wondering if something was wrong with me. This was one of the few times Google was my friend and didn't tell me I was going to die.

I read about other women who felt the same way I did. There were others who also no longer wanted any sort of physical affection. I learned it is a common symptom of pregnancy. Women can swing far one way, wanting all of the physical touch in the world, or they lean the absolute opposite direction. It was hard, especially because it was our first year of marriage, and I wanted Rafe to feel loved. I knew from *The 5 Love Languages* that he's a physical touch kind of person, always wanting a hug or to hold hands. There were times I didn't want a hug or even to sit close to him on the couch. I still had to push through and do so anyway. Loving someone isn't about what they can give us but rather about how we can love them. It's about putting them before ourselves.

Ouch

I'd heard somewhere that people say hurtful things to you when you're pregnant. You don't want to believe that is true. I'm sorry to be the bearer of bad news, but it is. I was "showing" larger than average while I was pregnant. So much so that when I would order maternity clothes, I couldn't order in my pre-pregnancy size. They did not fit me at all. Then there was the added stress and frustration of having to do all of my shopping on-line. I mean, it is great for some aspects of life, but not for maternity clothes. I wanted to go into a store and try things on, not return things over and over because of having to order a larger size. On top of being insecure about my changing body, I had to combat what people would say.

"Are you sure you're not having twins?"
"Hopefully you'll have your baby by twenty-six weeks so you don't get much bigger."
"I'm sure a tent could fit you."
"Oh, you're so sensitive; it's the hormones."
"You're so weighty, remember what you looked like in your wedding dress?"

Did your mouth just drop? Can you relate? These words stung. I've never been one that's quick on my feet, able to fire back with something witty. I just stayed silent or walked away in tears, shocked that people could say such cruel things. I'm now thankful I am that way, or I would have said something I'd regret in retaliation. For these words first stunned me, then made me cry, and third, made me angry. They caused division in relationships. The old rhyme we often learn as a child failed me: "Sticks and stones may break my bones, but words will never hurt me." It's an absolute lie.

Proverbs 18:21 says, "The tongue can bring death or life." None of those comments or questions brought me life. I know none of those people were trying to hurt my feelings, and I had to remind myself of that often. Not that my work toward forgiveness or understanding made it all okay, but I knew the pain wasn't intentional. They were all people who loved me. But as time went on, there was still bitterness in my heart toward them. I realized I had three choices.

1. Stuff these comments and questions deep down
2. Be angry at them and shut them out
3. Pray

So I chose to pray—hard. Oh, how I wanted to stay angry. I wanted to retaliate and give those people the silent treatment or a piece of my mind. However, I've learned in my walk with God that what He asks us to do isn't always what we want to do. Meaning, I chose option three. I prayed. I chose to be like Jesus and to not let the bitterness in my heart win. I prayed that God would heal the pain caused by those words. I prayed that God would help me forgive the people who said them. It reminds me of Matthew 18:21–22:

Then Peter came to Jesus and asked, "Lord,

how many times shall I forgive my brother or
sister who sins against me? Up to seven times?"
Jesus answered, "I tell you, not seven times, but
seventy-seven times."

We are called to forgive one another. Not just to say, "*I forgive you,*" but to fully forgive from the heart.

I reached a place where I forgave them, but sometimes, when I revisit the hurtful words in my memory, it's still hard. I have to forgive them over and over. It's not always an easy one-time process where you flip the switch and it's all good. Their words . . . I don't know if I'll ever forget them. But they are not words that I've let define me. Nor are they words I cling to.

There's nothing the enemy wants more than to cause division in relationships, and I will not let him win. More than that, I can now see the blessing in those horrible words. Hard to believe, right?

Throughout life, whether pregnant or not, people will say things that hurt our feelings. The piercing words or messages often come from the people we love most. We can't control what people say, but we can control how we react to them. I used to react with my temper. I learned in counseling that there are primary and secondary emotions. A secondary emotion can be anger, shame, or jealousy, and responding from those emotions is not advisable. A primary emotion goes deeper than that; it's how we truly feel: hurt, hopeless, or helpless. I learned to express my feelings from that deeper place. I had to practice to be more vulnerable and not get riled up by being misunderstood.

Over time, this practice taught me self-control, which is one of the fruits of the spirit (Galatians 5:22–23). Everything we go through can be used for God's glory. It can be used to make us become more like Jesus. To sharpen us. I didn't see it then, but I see it now. God defines me—not others—and He strengthens me through the difficulties I face.

A Deeper Dive Into Sensitivity

I want to dig a little deeper into one of the comments since it was the hardest for me to overcome. "Oh, you're so sensitive; it's the hormones." The word *sensitive* in my family is a fighting word. I've been told to *stop being so sensitive* for most of my life. Because of this, I learned that sensitivity is a negative trait, not a positive one.

One day (when I wasn't pregnant), Rafe told me I was being sensitive, and I felt a heat rise within me as I started to glare at him. He looked at me, confused. I explained to him why I thought it was a cruel thing to say. He told me he thought being sensitive was a beautiful quality. "We need people to be sensitive to others. It's a sign of empathy and compassion. Amazingly, you can express emotion when others find it difficult to do."

After some thought, I agreed. If you're feeling sensitive or have been labeled "sensitive," I hope you see it as a word to be celebrated, not belittled by.

The Maternity Photos

Before heading back to London from our babymoon, we took maternity photos. I was terrible throughout my pregnancy at remembering to take weekly or monthly "bump" photos. I was either too tired and didn't want to get ready or forgetful. Plus, my inner critic told me that I just looked like I'd gained weight, not like I was pregnant.

I found it annoying how many people told me I "must do the bump photos" or I'd regret it. I don't know why people want to push their agendas on others. I'm a photographer. I know what photos I want and don't want, and I wanted people to stop pushing me to do them. But I never communicated what I wanted. I learned quickly that, throughout pregnancy, you smile and nod *a lot*.

It's true, though. I wanted the perfect picture to share on social media. It's hard when your body gains more weight than others' do. And when you tell people you're having a hard time with it, they just tell you how beautiful you are and dismiss your feelings, which doesn't help at all. It's okay that some days are harder than others.

Side note: It's okay to not take any photos, take a ton of photos, share them, or not. Be at peace with how you want to capture and share your season of pregnancy.

When we got home from the babymoon, I went to edit the photos from the maternity shoot. I remember my reaction when I first saw my thighs. *How have I not noticed them before? They're huge! When and where did they come from?* My dad used to call me "chicken legs" growing up. Mine were more like elephant legs now. I continued to struggle with the way my body was changing.

That was until I had a conversation with Nicole. She told me that my thighs needed to get bigger to support my baby, to carry the weight of him growing in my tummy. Once I learned the purpose of why they'd changed, my self-judgment vanished. So whatever you may be struggling with, find its purpose. I hope it will bring you peace like it did for me.

Prayer

God, thank You for the way You have designed our bodies—that You have put purpose in all things. I pray for our thoughts. I pray that we turn our focus to You. That You help us forgive those who say things that hurt our feelings. That You help us accept our bodies. That You help us see the purpose in change and growth. Whether it be a mental or physical change, You are teaching us so much about You. Open up our eyes to see the blessings You have given us. Help us express our emotions in healthy ways, knowing that we are never too much or too sensitive. You see us. You gave us our feelings, and whatever is from You is good. Remind us of that, Lord, in our most challenging moments. That You and Your Son have felt the same feelings we have, and it'll all be okay. In Jesus's name, Amen.

Mental Health Tip

Here is a mental exercise I do when my emotions are feeling all over the place. It helps bring in logical thoughts when it's hard to control my anxiety. I've used this tool—given to me by my counselor, Heather Harrison—for so long that I rarely need to look at the questions anymore. I hope it's a tool that helps you too! I've sent it to many women, so know this: you're not alone if you're facing anxiety.

Suggested questions to help you dispute anxious thoughts:

1. What is the evidence?
What evidence do I have to support my thoughts?

What evidence do I have against them?

2. What alternate views are there?

How might an outsider view this situation?

How would I have viewed it before anxiety?

3. How much does thinking this way cost me?

Does it help me or stop me from getting what I want?
How?

What might be the outcome of looking at things in a
healthier way?

4. Is my thinking realistic?
(pick the ones that pertain to you)

Am I thinking in all-or-nothing terms?

Am I condemning myself as a total person on the basis of
a single event?

Am I concentrating on my weaknesses and forgetting my
strengths?

Am I blaming myself for something that is not my fault?

Am I taking something personally which has little or nothing to do with me?

Am I expecting myself to be perfect?

Am I using a double standard? How would I view my best
friend in this situation?

Am I paying attention only to the bad side of things?

Am I overestimating the chances of disaster?

Am I exaggerating the importance of events?

Am I assuming I can do nothing to change my situation?

CHAPTER FOUR

I Am Beautiful

ACCEPTING MY BODY BY SEEING IT THROUGH GOD'S EYES

———

Rewind to 2018.

Welcome to my second date with Rafe! On day two of our initial meeting in Uganda, we preached in a church in a small village just outside of Kampala. The amount of dancing during worship there was incredible! I've never had such a workout in church. I could barely breathe when it was time for us to speak. It felt like I was in a cardio class at the gym. I remember the worship leader yelling, "Put your hands on your hips! Now, get low!" I hadn't "gotten low" for God before, but hey, it was a blast, and I was there for it! Sometimes, Christianity is taken so seriously, over-analyzed and over-organized to make sure people feel "comfortable." We can forget about having fun. Dancing, no matter how low you go, can give the Lord glory too.

When I was preparing for this message, I was nervous. It was my first time preaching. I sought out different mentors and pastors and asked how they prepare for their talks.

The advice I received was:

1. Know your audience; who are you speaking to?
2. What burden do you carry that you want to put on the shoulders of others?
3. Use your voice, knowing when to speak loudly and when to speak softly to draw people in.
4. Have three main points that you want to get across.
5. Always end with Jesus and the cross.

So I went to work on my sermon. It was on how we are made in the image of God and also the joy of comparison. Surprising, right? I've heard so many times from evangelical Christian pastors that comparison is the *thief of joy*. I don't completely disagree, but I do think it matters how you look at it. It's similar to the question, *do you see the glass half full or half empty?*

First, I answered points one and two—who is my audience, and what is the burden I carry? My audience was clear. They were a small church of Ugandans who knew Jesus. I decided to choose a topic based on one of the experiences I had in Uganda.

In 2014, while teaching at a school, during one of the breaks, some kids pushed me into the shade and said, "No, you don't want your skin to get dark like ours." It broke my heart. From that memory, I wanted to speak on comparison and what it means to compare. I wanted to share how God sees all of his children as beautiful. That we're all unique and made in his image. I've always hoped for everyone to come together, find the commonalities that join us, and celebrate our differences. I started to realize this wasn't just a message for a small group of people in Uganda; it was a message I needed to hear too. Comparison was a topic I struggled with on many levels.

The next piece of advice was about using my voice. Well, you can only do so much when you have a translator. But I was thankful that my Ugandan brother, Joshua, was translating for us. Joshua has such a peaceful presence, and he believed God would use me to speak to His people. He helped give me the confidence I needed to be on that stage. He also knew me so well that I trusted what he translated would be true to what I was trying to say and, ultimately, what God was saying through me. Having a translator also helped me slow down, and that slower speed put my emotions at ease. While I was still stateside preparing for this sermon, so many thoughts of self-doubt had come into my head before traveling:

- What makes you think you're qualified? You didn't go to Bible college.
- What makes you think you can relate to these people?
- You're in your early twenties; do you really think you have wisdom?

I messaged Joshua and told him that maybe I shouldn't do a sermon. I wasn't even a pastor. I can still hear his return voice note saying, "You are a mighty woman of God, coming in the name of the Lord. He has put a word on your heart. Because of Him, you are qualified." Standing on that stage with Joshua was such a comfort because he didn't just believe in me, he believed that God could speak through me to His people. God knew I needed Josh standing up there with me. To have Rafe up there as well was such a blessing. It filled my heart with joy and put me in awe of God as the One who was answering the desires of my heart. It was a glimpse of what life could be like in ministry together, something I hoped and dreamed of doing with my husband one day.

Public speaking used to be my biggest fear. Growing up and attending school, I would tremble when I had to talk in front of the classroom. Having my face turn bright red and feeling hot never helped. After each time I spoke, I doubted myself, thinking I talked too fast or what I said wasn't clear enough. I put myself down over and over, giving in to the fear and not even seeking the truth.

Nonetheless, God kept putting the desire in my heart to preach, which was confusing to me. But I wanted to be up there; I wanted to tell my story of how Jesus changed my life, and I wanted to explain the gospel in a gentle, authentic way. I wanted to connect with people and have God use me. I said the prayer, "God, I'm willing for You to send me. I'll do what You ask me to do."

It's not always the easiest prayer because then you actually do have to listen. God responded. He kept creating opportunities for me to preach. I've slowly spoken to bigger and bigger groups of people over the years—not that the number of people in the room matters to me. It showed me that we have a loving Father who isn't going to throw us in the deep end and say, "Okay, now learn how to swim." He'll ease us into what He has planned for us. Remember, sometimes our fears can be indicators of what exactly God is calling us to do. It's our choice to either be someone who stops themselves from living out God's plans or someone who trusts in Him enough to try.

Now to the main points I wanted to get across. (You're basically getting my sermon notes.) I started with Scripture.

"Imitate God, therefore, in everything you do, because you are his dear children. Live a life filled with love, following the example of Christ. He loved us and offered himself as a sacrifice for us, a pleasing aroma to God" (Ephesians 5:1–2).

So, what is the definition of image? Using the Bible and an online dictionary, I came up with these:

- *Genesis 1:27 says, "So God created man in His own image; in the image of God He created him; male and female He created them."*
- *A physical likeness or representation of a person.*
- *A mental representation or idea.*

Therefore, if we are made in God's image, it doesn't just mean our looks. It means to be like, think like, give like, serve like, lead like, and love like God. God sent His Son as a representation, to show us how to be like God in our daily lives. If we're honest with ourselves, we often take our eyes off Jesus and look to others. We scroll through Instagram to see what kind of pictures people are posting. We wish our life could be more like theirs. We do all these other things instead of choosing the joy of comparison, which comes from doing our best to be like Jesus. Unfortunately, we often choose the sin of comparison, which is idolatry.

What is *idolatry*? According to Lexico, the Oxford dictionary, it's defined as the following:

• *Extreme admiration, love, or reverence for something or someone*

Let there be no sexual immorality, impurity, or greed among you. Such sins have no place among God's people. Obscene stories, foolish talk, and coarse jokes—these are not for you. Instead, let there be thankfulness to God. You can be sure that no immoral, impure, or greedy person will inherit the Kingdom of Christ and of God. For a greedy person is an idolater, worshiping the things of this world (Ephesians 5:3–5).

Sounds a bit intense, right? It's easy to point out other people tangled in the comparison game or those who worship things of the world, but it's not so easy to stare in the mirror and realize you do the same. Sometimes, it's an unconscious choice. We don't even realize we are desiring to be more like someone else, and we travel far from the person God created us to be. When we reach Heaven, I don't think God will say, "Why weren't you more like (insert name here)?" When we try to be like others, we go against God's Creation. We miss out on the beauty we have to give to the world.

When I was writing those sermon notes, I didn't think that four years later, they'd help me in motherhood. That sermon was one I needed before I became pregnant, while I was pregnant, and in postpartum.

When I was pregnant and struggling with my changing body, I'd make the mistake of idolizing old photos—old versions—of myself. Even in postpartum, it was hard to escape the wedding photographs we had hanging in our home. I'd either compare myself to how I used to look, missing some aspect of my body, or I'd think to myself, "Wow, why was I so mean to her? Why was I so hard on myself back then? Why didn't I enjoy the body I used to have?"

To be honest, I'm still struggling with my body. With these hips and tummy that I've never had before. Sometimes, I still look at others and compare myself to them: *Look at how her body has bounced back faster than mine*, I hear in my head. Then, using questions, I remind myself to be kind: Who told me my body needs to be back in shape immediately, and why? Why can't I look at my body and think, *Wow, you have done so much for me! You have kept me healthy, sustained me, and created a miracle in me.* I often wonder why it's so hard for me to comprehend that I'm still living a healthy lifestyle, and that that's more important than the size of my jeans.

Who is telling me I need to look a particular way? Who is telling me that I should look more like those other postpartum moms? I know at least one source. I took a break from social media because it just wasn't healthy for me—emotionally or mentally. Negative thoughts swirled in my mind, and I had to choose daily to look to God instead of those perfect images on my screen. I had to remind myself that I am created in His image and because of that alone, I am beautiful.

Today's media seems to be the loudest voice in defining what beauty is. We see it in movies and other mediums starting at such a young age. I struggled for a long time because I had not learned that beauty comes from God and thought instead it was defined by celebrities, the cool girls at school, or a boyfriend's validation.

Have you ever said out loud, "I am beautiful?" Not *to* someone, not *for* someone, but to yourself. Try it! Go into a room—just you alone—and declare it: "I am beautiful." How does it feel? For me, it was uncomfortable. Then, I thought, *Why?* Why is it hard for me to say that about myself? What does society tell me? What lies have I believed? What from my past have I accepted? What is my definition of *beauty*? I believe every person contains beauty—all of us! So I shouldn't have shame in saying it, and neither should you. There should be freedom and celebration when the word *beauty* leaves our lips. We are as beautiful as both the sunrise and the sunset. We are God's most precious creation.

So please do me a favor. Practice this. Practice saying it aloud until you believe it: "I am beautiful." Don't doubt it; get uncomfortable until you find comfort in the fact that you are beautiful. Because God created you.

Side note: If you're still having trouble with that, think about this: How do you want your own

child to speak to themselves? Hopefully, that
question can motivate you to be kinder to your-
self. It did for me.

If you are struggling with your body, looks, thoughts, relationships, job, or motherhood, start living a life of comparing yourself to Jesus. You have to know Who you come from to know who you can become. I challnge you to learn more about the lifestyle of Jesus. If you don't know much about Him, I recommend you start with reading one of the gospels. I promise you'll find the joy of comparison when you align yourself with the right person. Striving to be like Jesus will bring you joy. Remember: try not to be so hard on yourself. Our culture is already trying to tell you how to think and who to be.

It's always your choice whom to believe.

Scripture to Dwell On

"Do not let your adornment be merely outward—arranging the hair, wearing gold, or putting on fine apparel—rather let it be the hidden person of the heart, with the incorruptible beauty of a gentle and quiet spirit, which is very precious in the sight of God." (1 Peter 3:3–4)

"The eye is the lamp of the body. If your eyes are healthy, your whole body will be full of light. But if your eyes are unhealthy, your whole body will be full of darkness. If then the light within you is darkness, how great is that darkness!" (Matthew 6:22–23)

"Therefore I tell you, do not worry about your life, what you will eat or drink; or about your body, what you will wear. Is not life more than food, and the body more than clothes?" (Matthew 6:25)

CHAPTER FIVE

Stick a Fork In it; I'm Done!

MOVING TO SCOTLAND AND FINAL PREPARATIONS

———

Living in London was amazing and difficult all at once. I didn't think I'd miss it until we moved away. The community and friends we had there were incredible. Being there during the lockdown was difficult, but we still enjoyed some sweet moments.

One of our sweetest friends, Roz, would drop by our window with cinnamon rolls or just come to chat and ask how we were doing. From Joe Baxter singing outside our window until we'd open it to say hello to Will and Jenn dropping off pancake mix and dried fruit early in the mornings, it was a lovely community. James and Susannah checked in to see how we were, and Pat Allerton sat by our window with a cup of tea while it poured rain outside.

How amazing it is when you get to live near people you love. That was the best part of our little flat. It may have been small, but it was worth staying in that tight, cramped space to live within a stone's throw of our church community and in our close-knit neighborhood.

There was another downside: we only lived near two parks. The one closest to us was nice, but how many days can you spend in the same tiny park? You may recognize the other by name: Hyde Park. It is one of the most beautiful parks in England, and it's huge. It was usually so crowded that it often gave me anxiety to simply walk there. Plus, it was getting harder and harder for me to walk long distances because my hands were starting to swell in pain.

Feeling trapped in our flat, I started to pray to be back in the mountains. To be near nature and able to step outside and smell the fresh air. When I lived in Oregon, I used to hike every weekend. I always wanted to explore a new trail. Not having been in any forested nature for months, I started to crave the outdoors more and more. I wondered, *Where is a beautiful place we can visit that isn't too far away?*

Instantly, Scotland popped into my mind. I had always dreamed of photographing the Scottish Isles. Not like that would be easy being pregnant, but still, a girl could dream. After that daydream went on for a bit, Rafe was told by his company that there was the possibility he would be "made redundant." Any hopes of making a trip to Scotland came crashing down. We needed to save money in case he was let go from his job.

For some reason, even though he was told he could be let go, we had an overwhelming sense of peace. This seemed quite strange given that I was already in my third trimester. I mean, I was about to have a baby, and my husband might potentially lose his job in a country where we had no right to stay without one. So, yes—having peace was surprising. The only source it could have come from was God.

Early in my pregnancy, someone told me, "The only thing you can carry is your baby." Meaning, I couldn't carry stress, people's emotions, or anything else. Everything should be focused on my baby and free from negativity. I would tell myself that often if I started to get stressed or anxious.

"The only thing I can carry is my baby."

The words helped me mentally. I even told Rafe, "I love you, but during this time, I can't carry your emotions." This may sound a bit rude, but I needed him to find another outlet—a friend or pastor to talk to.

Side note: This was one example of why it's so important to have friends and family around you, select people you can go to and be completely transparent with. Friends that won't judge you but do want the best for you and your marriage. Remember, if the only thing you can carry right now is your baby, that's okay.

A week after finding out Rafe might be let go from his project and me letting go of my Scottish Isle daydream, he got a call from his line manager. I watched his face go from serious to smiling to laughing. He noticed my confusion about what was happening, so he asked the person on the other end of the phone to hold.

"Cait, they want us to relocate to a new project in Scotland."

I just started laughing alongside Rafe. Back on the phone, he told them, "No, I don't need to talk it over with my wife; she's fine with it." He knew my laughter was a yes.

After the call, I asked what the job was, and he explained that he'd be working for Highlands and Islands Airports of Scotland, with no need to even do an interview. I mean, when does that happen? We savored the gift because it seemed God had already been preparing us to move. He was already giving us peace, planting ideas in our minds, and filling our hearts with specific desires. I love the way God works. That cheeky Guy. I can imagine Jesus laughing alongside us.

Saying Goodbye

After Rafe had officially accepted the job in Scotland, it was time to tell people about the move. I knew the only way I'd leave my job at St. Peter's Notting Hill would be if God had us move. This job had been such a huge blessing to me in so many ways. It was the reason I'd been able to stay in the UK because they had sponsored my visa. It was my first time working in ministry. It's where I gained confidence in preaching. I learned much from this job, and Rafe and I both loved the people in our church. They had truly become our family away from family.

When I first moved to London to date Rafe, I told God, "If You want me to stay, then You'll have to provide the job and the place I'll live." This had been especially true since I was only able to be there for six months on a tourist visa at the time. Right before I headed back to the states for Christmas in 2018, I was offered a position as the children's pastor and assisting with media communications at St. Peter's—a job tailored to my heart and passions.

I had such faith and a belief that London was where God wanted me that I booked my tickets back to London in January 2019 even without a working visa. Amazingly, my visa was approved in five days, which you know is unheard of if you're familiar with the system.

I knew ministry would be my next step, but I didn't know what that would look like. It was clear that God had opened the door to London in the first place, and so I only felt peace leaving for Scotland now because God said it was time. And what an incredible way to leave!

It was hard to leave because I had grown so much spiritually while I was there. It's amazing how much your faith grows in new places and through new experiences.

Everyone supported us when we shared the news of our departure. We even had a sendoff service, socially distanced of course, just for us. It was the most beautiful service I'd experienced—something I'll never forget. Both Rafe and I were in awe of the love we felt. I believe every job is a stepping stone to something God wants to teach us to carry on into the next season. Thank you, Pat Allerton, for trusting me, believing in me, being a go-to vicar for all things theological, launching us into this next chapter, and giving such a special sermon to send us off. We'll cherish that memory and will always be thankful for the time we spent doing ministry together.

Scotland Bound

Before moving to Scotland, we were given two choices: we could live in Glasgow or Edinburgh. We ended up choosing Edinburgh because we had so many friends that had gone to university there. If you haven't seen photographs of the city before, I suggest searching Edinburgh online. It's a gorgeous town. I've also learned it's rare for an American to know how to pronounce it, so I'm going to quickly sound it out for you: *Ed-in-bruh*. Now, if you ever visit, you'll sound less like a tourist.

Rafe's new manager wanted us to move in December, but with my due date being November 22, we asked if we could move sooner. If not, we'd be moving to a new city with a newborn in the middle of winter. No, thank you!

Thankfully, they agreed, and we transitioned from England to Scotland in mid-September. Before we moved "up north," we ended up staying with our friends Tommaso and Maddalena along with our godson George for two weeks in their home in London. We had to get out of our flat so the new tenants could move in, and I had one more doctor's appointment in town. You know people are friends for life when you can be in lockdown together and love every moment. They ended up watching our plants for over a month before we found a place to live in Scotland. Yes, for over a month, we lived in an Airbnb in Scotland until we found a place to call home. Thankfully, the Airbnb had a bathtub, or it would have been rough!

Moving to a city we'd never been to before was stressful, especially being pregnant. If I haven't mentioned it enough, the third trimester is difficult. I was basically either working remotely, in the bathtub, bouncing on my pregnancy ball, or looking at homes. As I'm sure you know, looking for a place to live is absolutely exhausting. I'm pretty sure I could have become a leasing agent with the knowledge of Edinburgh I had gained.

After a few weeks went by, we had to move to another Airbnb, and I started to get discouraged. I told

God all about it. "God, why haven't you found us a place yet?" I lamented. It was such a competitive market that if we weren't the first ones to see it, then we probably weren't going to get it. Places were going so fast, and that produced extra pressure to say yes to anything. We one-time viewed a place with another couple. At the end of the viewing, the seller's agent told us that the first one to call the office would get the house. Both couples started frantically calling once we got to our cars, then Rafe and I thought, *Wait, what? What are we doing?*

We hadn't even liked that place. The inside had a weird smell, and there was no natural lighting. We were so desperate to have a home, we weren't even thinking. We were trying so hard to move in somewhere that we didn't stop to involve God in any step of the process.

Mentors for the Win

At that point, I received some advice from my mentor, Nicole. She called me to check in, and once I updated her with our housing dilemma, she said, "Why don't you sit down with God, close your eyes, and envision what your home will be like." *Huh*, I thought. I'd never done that before, so I thought I'd try it.

Side note: I was taught to have someone above you (a mentor), beside you (Christian friends), and below you (people you mentor) (Proverbs 13:20). So, If you don't have a mentor in your life, I advise you to pray for one. Someone who has gone before you, that can see where you're going, that is cheering you on, praying for you, and encouraging you to become more like Jesus.

Once we got off the phone, I hobbled over and plopped on the uncomfortable Airbnb couch. Absolutely exhausted from life and pregnancy as I lay down, I felt like I just needed to surrender my timing. That we'd stay in this small rental until it was the right time for us to go. To let go of my less-than-ideal circumstance and be thankful we had a place to stay for now. As I closed my eyes, I tried to imagine one of the beautiful Edinburgh flats we'd seen online and visited. The ones with the tall ceilings and elegant crown moldings. But I couldn't see anything. I couldn't even picture one, even though we'd just been to a half-dozen places like that.

All I could imagine was a house with a nursery, a garden, and a guest room so we could host family and friends. I envisioned a living room big enough to have people over for dinner, despite the fact that social gatherings were still limited during a pandemic. I still had hope. It was an absolute dream home, and I asked God if it was possible. After all, we didn't have the money for a place like that, especially when I had moved to maternity pay.

Over the next few days, more viewings went by but nothing came close to what I had dreamed about with God. Rafe and I said no to places that could have worked but that we didn't have peace about. Sometimes, you have to say no to the good to say yes to the great. *Great must be around the corner*, we thought.

While praying that God would sort this out, our friend Kerrie introduced us to some of her friends in Scotland via Facebook messenger. They were so kind, and we planned a walk to go on with them—the number one activity of pandemic life.

Rafe messaged them to ask if they knew of anyone renting or moving out of their place. One individual responded quickly. "We know a pastor that is moving up north and planning on renting his home. If you're interested, I can put you in contact."

"Sounds too good to be true!" This new friend-of-a-friend kindly connected us with Euan and arranged for us to have a viewing of his home with his father-in-law since he was already up in the highlands.

The day arrived, and as we walked inside the house, I knew it was the one. The God-ordained one. It was everything I had dreamed about with God; it just needed a fresh coat of paint. It wasn't ready to be moved into right away. The homeowner wanted to make sure all inspections were done, which we so appreciated. When we finally met with Euan about signing the lease, he told us they were thinking about selling the house but decided first to pray for a young Christian couple that might want to rent from them. I mean, *hello!* Here we are! God had answered two prayers at once.

After we signed the paperwork to rent, Euan prayed for us. It was a powerful reminder of the relationships that we have as brothers and sisters in Christ even with strangers. God provided for us through this home in every way possible: a nursery by our room, a lounge to host dinners (one day), and a basement that led to the back garden with a guest bed and bathroom. Don't be afraid to pray for specific things with God. It's so incredible when he shows up within the details.

Nesting

We signed the paperwork and moved in, then nested like crazy. I've never liked the term *nesting*, although it's the only one I know to use. Rafe and I were both in a "let's get this home ready for our baby" mode. I'd never cleaned so much in my life. Rafe painted, and we went to every furniture store in and around the city of Edinburgh. Thankfully, they were still open in the pandemic, but I'm pretty sure everyone else was redoing or redecorating their homes, too—which was unfortunate for us, because every sofa we looked at had a fifteen-to-seventeen-week backorder. *I can't not have a sofa when I have a baby*, I thought. We ended up ordering a "sofa in a box" that came three days later, and it worked out perfectly. It was not the coziest of sofas, and I didn't like its teal color, but it fit in our space and did the job.

I talk about paint and a sofa, but we really did have to start from scratch. For those who don't know, London flats often come fully furnished. When I lived there, it was rare to find a place that wasn't furnished. This meant we moved to Scotland with our clothes, a few rugs, some dishes, and our wedding gifts. That was about it.

My favorite part of the nesting, though, was getting our baby's nursery ready. We kept it simple and went with a lovely wallpaper that carried a woodland theme.

Another positive aspect of pandemic life was being able to work remotely. It's just not a common perk for a job at a church. Working for a church is all about building relationships and community. It was an absolute blessing to be able to move from London and still do communications and children's ministry while in Edinburgh. The hardest part was continuing "Story Time With Cait." I would film myself reading a story from a children's Bible, talking about what the passage meant, and at the end, I would say a prayer for the kids. I loved it, but when my face started to change (a.k.a., get fuller and rounder), it got harder for me to do. New insecurities emerged, particularly one about my nose getting wider and wider. Although, in truth, my entire body had slowly started to swell. I was also waking up with pain from carpal tunnel, had difficulty rolling over, and had a constantly stuffy nose, night sweats, little fists punching my ribs, insane dreams, and a very swollen face. I thought I was going to be able to work up until our baby boy was born, but that just wasn't the case. It had all started becoming too much, too uncomfortable, and I was unable to focus.

I know I've just made pregnancy sound super glamourous. Some Instagram accounts make it look like it is, but it was a lot harder than everyone had ever told me or admitted to. It was beautiful but hard.

So what are a few things I learned?

- To get ready *for myself*.
- To do my hair, maybe a splash of makeup *for myself*.
- To put on a cute outfit; well, let's just say jeans instead of sweats *for myself*.
- To take pictures of my bump *for myself* and Rafe, as he loved documenting this journey.
- To pursue God more than ever *for myself*.
- To be kind *to myself*.

What I learned was that it does help to "get ready" from time to time. Pregnancy was tiring, but when I got ready it made me feel good, and it helped me mentally.

I was growing a human. No matter how big my nose grew, how sore my hands and back became . . . I knew I would do it all again for him.

Everything in life has a cost. The cost of pregnancy, I believe, isn't talked about much. My friends and family told me about how amazing and beautiful it was but . . . I didn't find everything about it beautiful. It was really challenging at times. When you think about it, would something be as treasured if there wasn't a cost for it? Would things that matter be as treasured without the trials we face to get them? Maybe for me, I needed a swollen nose to remind me of where my beauty comes from. Now, looking back, I can see the purpose in all of the struggles and understand that my body was creating a safe space for my baby.

Side note: Don't cut your hair in your third trimester. I got mine cut and thinned because it was driving me nuts. Six months later, it started falling out. Oh, the joys!

Scottish Perks

As I started to hit a brick wall in my pregnancy, I registered for a Scottish Baby Box. What is that, you may ask? The Scottish government sends registered pregnant women a gift box. But it's not just any gift box. It's a box with major goodies, including a mattress for your baby. And boy, did we use that box! It was filled with baby clothes, a blanket, a bath towel, a baby wrap, toys, bibs, a thermometer, nursing pads, and more—everything you need for the early days with your baby. I was in awe of the range of gifts. I never thought the Scottish government could make me feel so loved. One of my favorite items in the box was a poem that we ended up framing for the nursery. Get ready. I've included a few lines to read out loud. (Rafe does a pretty good job with a Scottish accent; I still sound as American as ever!)

"Welcome Wee One" by Professor Jackie Kay CBE

O ma darlin wee one
At last you are here in the wurld
And wi' aa your wisdom
Your een bricht as the stars,
You've filled this hoose with licht,
Yer trusty wee haun, your globe o' a heid,
My cherished yin, my hert's ain!

How special is that? It melted my heart.

Preparing for the Birth

Giving birth is not like in the movies; if the movies matched real life, we'd be watching very lengthy, intense birth scenes. My sister's experiences giving birth to my amazing niece and nephew gave me somewhat of a realistic expectation of what my hospital stay would be like. Well, for a hospital in America anyway.

After she had given birth, my sister had a private room where her husband could stay the night and family could visit. In the UK, you can have that option if you want to pay for it—in London, at least. I'm not even sure they offer that kind of room or privacy in Scotland.

The Royal Edinburgh Infirmary was the hospital located closest to us. There was a birth center there where you could choose to have a water birth, which was an incredible option. We learned ahead of time that Rafe could drop me off in front of the hospital when I started having contractions, but he couldn't come in until I arrived in my room. Then, from there, he could be with me for the entire birth, but only until one to two hours after. Then, he would be asked to leave, and there were no visiting hours. Not only that, but I couldn't get a private room. I would be placed in a room with three to four other women and their babies. I didn't know how I felt about all of that. Rafe's auntie assured me that it was a special experience to be around other women who were going through the same thing. She told us that she had made some of her closest friends in the labor ward.

We'll see, I thought. I was most saddened by the thought of being without Rafe. I couldn't understand why my husband wasn't able to visit me and our baby after the birth. It was difficult to try to keep calm during the weeks leading up to the due date.

The Birth Plan

With learning what the hospital was going to be like came the need to create a birth plan. I'm happy I did because it gave me confidence. It made me feel like I knew what I was about to do, even though I absolutely didn't. There were countless birth plans and articles online. I could have read them, but I'm a visual learner.

Thankfully, Zoe—from our NCT group—was reading *The Positive Birth Book* by author Milli Hill. It includes visual birth plan icons that you can cut out and glue on some paper, which I think is much easier for nurses, midwives, and doctors to see. I highly recommend checking it out. Looking through the icons helped me learn more about the birth process, determine what questions I had, and see what I would need to research more about. It also made me think about what my specific plan would be since I had tested positive with Strep B. I planned how, if, and when I was going to be put on antibiotics down to the most minute details, including in which arm I wanted the IV. I have friends who are nurses and was able to ask loads of questions when it came to Strep B.

However you decide to give birth is your choice. I hope you don't feel pressured to do it a certain way because that's what all your friends have done. I suggest learning about all the options for yourself. You'll know what's right for you and your baby. This is a chance to start trusting those motherly instincts.

For me, I wasn't ready to do a home birth. It was my first baby, and I was a bit too nervous, worried about everything that could go wrong. Plus, I had no idea what to expect. I felt safer going to the hospital. However, I still wanted to try to labor in water, especially since I had been dreaming of being in a pool throughout the coronavirus lockdown. If for some reason that didn't work out and I needed an epidural, I was open to that. And if that didn't work out and I had to get a cesarean section (C-section), I would be open to that too. That was certainly not my first choice, but I wanted to have plans A, B, and C in the event things changed and spiraled out of my control. I hoped my planning would help me flow with the changes because I would be semi-prepared for them. It's kind of like when you decide you're going to go to a Mexican restaurant, and then randomly you discover it's closed, and you have to go to an Italian place instead. It's likely not going to be as good because you already had your mind set on what you wanted to eat. But if you had a plan B already in place for the Italian restaurant, your expectations aren't as dashed—or so it seems. Okay, so that comparison might be a bit of a stretch, but I hope you understand my point. It's better to be flexible than to feel let down by reality and unmet expectations, especially during labor.

I wanted a water birth, but now I also knew who would be in the room and what their role was for a C-section. That's my advice: prepare for what you hope for but hold loosely to it. Things might change, and if they do, you'll be ready for it. Another thing to be ready for is how you're going to get to the hospital. Something that was suggested to us was to do a test drive to the hospital a couple of times to check different routes, to see which would be fastest at what times of the day, and to find alternatives to use in the event of traffic or road work. This was immensely valuable for us to do. Not only because we were living in a new city, but also because we learned that one of the main roads in front of the park near us was closed on weekends. Our first time doing the test drive, we went to the wrong hospital! We thought we were driving to Edinburgh Royal infirmary; instead, we drove to The Royal Edinburgh Hospital, which we learned is a psychiatric hospital. We laughed so hard about ending up there that I thought I started having contractions! If it had turned out I was, I don't think I would have been laughing anymore. When I told our midwife about it, she said that would have been a very interesting place to have a baby!

I'm going to outline my birth planning checklist below. You may have googled this already and have everything sorted out. If not, here are a few tips:

My Third Trimester Checklist

• Go on a babymoon. Celebrate (and mourn) the change in lifestyle that's to come.

- Install a car seat in your car or have a plan for how you're going to get one to the hospital after the baby arrives.
- Drive to the hospital a few times, trying a couple of routes, just in case there's traffic on the big day.
- Have a place ready for your baby to sleep.
- Get onesies with mittens.
- Pick out a special baby outfit for when you take your newborn home from the hospital.
- Pack diapers/nappies and wipes.
- Prep some food and put it in the freezer or have a meal train set up through friends/family so they can drop off food at convenient times. Oh, and remind them not to make anything spicy . . . and you can only eat so much lasagna. Gift cards are great, too, if people ask how they can help. But food. Always food.
- Pack a large water bottle. For breastfeeding mommas, I was advised to drink two-thirds of my weight in ounces each day. Check with your healthcare provider.
- Think about postpartum care items such as pads and hot and cold packs for your vagina/breasts. Even if you have a cesarean, it still swells down there.
- Get your house professionally cleaned if you can afford to do so.
- Print/write out your birth plan.
- Think about a "going home plan." In case I had to stay at the hospital overnight, I had a list of things I wanted Rafe to do while he was home. These things included doing the laundry, vacuuming, and putting new sheets

on the bed. It was surprisingly helpful. If your husband can stay with you in the hospital, consider asking family members or friends to do these things for you.

• Don't forget a nightgown. I packed three comfy ones that were easy to breastfeed with. Consider using a cozy bathrobe. Sometimes, it's easier to wear them and skip the effort of getting dressed.

• Don't forget your hospital bag and slippers.

• Wash all of the baby clothes in unscented laundry detergent with no fabric softener beforehand.

• Think about how you'll handle your baby's baths.

• Watch love movies or do other things that spark that chemical, oxytocin, especially toward the end. It gets labor going. If you don't know what oxytocin is, I suggest reading about it.

• Use relaxing massage oil, and perhaps ask your husband to rub your back, legs, and feet with it.

• Buy a waterproof mattress cover for your bed and the baby's bed. With the night sweats that come after having a baby and the accidents your baby can have, they are priceless items. Think blowouts and poop everywhere. Make sure nothing happens to your mattress. You'll sleep better for it. Also, who knows where your water is going to release.

• Go get a pregnancy massage; you and your baby will love it. I was surprised how much our baby kicked during it. So, maybe it was not so relaxing, but it was special.

• Buy batteries, mainly because you never know when

you'll need them or what baby toys, pumps, or swings will need.

• On that note, consider getting a breast pump so you don't have to think about getting it later.

• Get a Haakaa, trust me.

• You also don't need a monitor yet, since newborns stay in your room, but if you want to get all the baby essentials now, then go for it. I suggest getting a monitor system that isn't just connected to your phone. We got one that is, and my phone is always dying.

• Find a book to start reading to your tummy. Your baby can hear your voice now, which is so special. Rafe read a children's Bible to our son almost every night.

• Learn and practice positions that can help during labor. I loved putting my arm around Rafe's neck and leaning on him.

• Download a book on tape. You can only watch so many movies.

• If you can afford to buy a robot vacuum cleaner, do it. They're not cheap, so we got ours on Black Friday, and we use it all of the time. It really has been helpful.

• Set up one group text for family and one for friends . . . for any of the people you want to give updates to.

• Give your husband a list of things to do—his own birth plan. He's in charge of making sure the car is ready, having snacks packed, messaging family and friends, and being your biggest advocate.

• Buy a stroller/pram and put it together in advance.

• Decide on additional things, such as a birth or new-born photographer. Sometimes, you have to book them far in advance.

Stroller Considerations

• How does it fold down?
• How do we store it, and does it work for our space?
• Is it just for use in the city or for hikes too?
• Do we plan on having more kids? If yes, is it compatible with that decision?
• Do I want to run with my pram?
• Is there a bundle deal online?
• Do I just want to buy one secondhand?
• Is it only compatible with one car seat, which I'll also have to buy?

I hope the lists above were helpful, and I likely missed some things. I'm sure this isn't the first or only list you're going to look at. Most of the bullet points are standard. However, the next list is more unique, and I hope you take the time to sit down and discuss it all with your husband.

• How are we going to deal with sleep deprivation?
• What are the roles of family members?
• What boundaries do we want to put in place for family and friends?

- How will we tackle night waking and feedings?
- What does self-care look like for each of us?
- How will we know if our mental health is suffering, and how will we best talk about it?
- What will we do with any downtime?
- What is our support system, and who will we let in for which circumstances?
- How will we make time for each other and love one another after our baby arrives?

Prayer

"Teach us to number our days, that we may gain a heart of wisdom." (Psalm 90:12)

Lord, we stop to thank You. Thank You for providing us with everything we need. I know I laid out a list of things to check off, but really, all we need is You. We surrender it all to You. I pray for each new momma that she would not feel overwhelmed by lists, articles, or books, especially this book. I pray she only feels loved and confident. I pray for wisdom as she and her spouse plan and prepare. I pray that their hearts overflow with joy, and in the darkest moments, You hug them with tender care. I wish I could love and support each new mom. I know how difficult it can be at times. Since I can't, I'm thankful that You can—and will. That You're always there. That You are our Source of love. That You are steadfast and never-changing. God, give us the strength we need today and wisdom for what's ahead. Amen.

CHAPTER SIX

People Are Answered Prayers

A UNIQUE SUPPORT SYETEM, NEAR AND FAR

———

Two are better than one,
because they have a good return for their labor:
If either of them falls down,
one can help the other up.
But pity anyone who falls
and has no one to help them up.
Also, if two lie down together, they will keep warm.
But how can one keep warm alone?
Though one may be overpowered,
two can defend themselves.
A cord of three strands is not quickly broken.
(Ecclesiastes 4:9–12)

If you ever google "friendship Scriptures," I guarantee this one will pop up in your search. It's a fairly well-known one. Strangely, some Scriptures seem to become clichés since they're used so often. If you haven't read or heard these verses from Ecclesiastes before, then I hope you found them as powerful as I do.

Throughout my faith journey—and life journey in general—there have been times when I've had an abundance of friends surrounding me. Every day of the week was filled, and I would see or talk to a different friend. Other times in my life, I've felt like I had none. I moved "across the pond," and my friends were still in the US; a long-distance friendship is very different from a friendship with someone who lives nearby. A friend that you see at church every Sunday, one you can grab coffee with, or someone who can come over for dinner at the last minute—these relationships are forged by something special. These friends know your boyfriend or husband and see you two together. You are *known*.

There have been many times in my life that I've prayed specifically for different things, especially friendships. God has answered many of my prayers in the form of people and through people. People who have uplifted, supported, and loved me in times of utter loneliness. That's why this Scripture is so meaningful to me. I don't know how I would have gotten through a lot of trials in my life without the people God has blessed me with.

Two are better than one,
because they have a good return for their labor.

Now, I always imagined my 30th birthday to be a big, over-the-top celebration. I often made the joke that I wanted it to be on a yacht in some topical or Mediterranean Sea. Basking in the sun with my closest friends, relaxing together. Even though that daydream was no longer going to be possible, my husband still took my desire close to heart. Too close, in my opinion. He still planned a trip for us to go out on a boat, but on the River Forth in Scotland. It was a sweet gesture, but didn't turn out so great. Being in my third trimester, it wasn't easy to walk. I felt like if I made one wrong step I'd fall off the boat and sink to the bottom. I was stressed, cold, and uncomfortable. I really tried to make the best of it because it was so kind for Rafe to do everything he could to make my dream a reality. At least he brought fancy cheese and crackers to eat.

The boat ride isn't what made my birthday. What made my birthday was Rafe posting on Facebook (hiding it from me of course) our home address and asking people to send me a birthday card. Rafe managed to keep all the cards hidden from me until that day. I woke up, came downstairs, and saw 80 or more cards on our windowsill. It was better than anything I could have imagined. It was like all my family and friends from all around the world were with me. I ended up getting my over-the-top celebration after all. The person that made that possible was Rafe. He's my "two are better than one" – he encouraged and supported me, and he knew that the words of people I love would bring me strength. Strength that I needed for this final trimester.

If either of them falls down, one can help the other up.

There have been so many moments in my pregnancy and postpartum where I needed someone to help me up, someone to give me perspective outside the emotional storm that was preventing me from seeing any light. There were moments where I thought I couldn't do it anymore. I faced times when I thought I didn't want to be pregnant. "I'm so sick; this is so hard." For the first few months after having our son, whom we named Zeik, the healing process and being away from family were difficult for me. Many times, I wanted to give up and simply lie in bed, feeling helpless. Besides going on walks and spending time with God, I knew I needed to talk it out. I needed to vent to other mom friends who understood the struggle. People who didn't give advice but just listened. I needed those who wouldn't try to fix me.

My point is, if you feel this way, know that you're not alone. If you feel guilty or like a failure, hear me when I say that many of us have been there. Just don't stay there.

Phone a friend, take a walk, and pray. You'll get through this. I'm reaching out to you now. You're not alone.

Also, if two lie down together, they will keep warm. But how can one keep warm alone?

To reiterate, you're not alone, and this confirms that. Now, I don't often lie down with my friends—though sometimes, I do need that long, drawn-out hug, where we don't pull away for minutes. Or maybe, I just need to sit on the couch, sharing a cozy blanket. We can't take care of our babies if we're not taking care of ourselves. We must let others into our mess, no matter how out of control we feel. I pray against any shame that is trying to bring you down.

I found it interesting that many times on this journey, I wanted my mom. When I would stop and think about it, I'd realize that now, *I'm* that person for *Zeik*. I'm the one he wants. To be honest, that realization helped me be more empathetic toward him when he was fussy or I was tired. It made me feel loved and needed. However, it also told me I needed to be taken care of just as much as he did.

Though one may be overpowered,
two can defend themselves.
A cord of three strands is not quickly broken.

There's a secret mom club I never knew about. Once you become a mom, you become a part of it. Other moms start reaching out, not because they want to give advice (though some do), but because they want to be there with and for you. They know how straining it can be as a new mother, and they champion you to keep going. They will defend you and teach you how to advocate for your baby . . . and yourself. Man, oh man, I had no idea how much I'd have to advocate for Zeik. So welcome, new momma or momma-to-be, to this community. You are in the unspoken secret mom club, and that's not so secret. You will now be in awe of other moms, those who have more than one child, those who work, those who stay at home, and those who manage many things.

One step at a time, though. Remember: Don't compare. Just take notes on the ones who have gone before you. Be kind to yourself and find the women who are going to support you.

One thing I did before Zeik was born was to have Rafe reach out to my girlfriends to make me a video to watch during labor. I'm not sure why I thought I'd have time to watch it or thought I'd be relaxed enough to watch anything during that time. (I wasn't at all! Ha-ha!)

But I ended up watching it a week or so after having Zeik. There were some segments I had to skip because laughing hurt my stitches. It ended up being 51 minutes long, 51 precious minutes of friends encouraging me, singing for me, sharing memories of our time together, dancing to "Push It," and praying for me. I didn't know how much I was going to need that video. I was too exhausted to call or talk much during the first few weeks home with Zeik, but watching that video gave me strength. I was able to use their tangible love to help me get out of bed when I couldn't do it on my own. Even though I had asked Rafe to ask my friends to create it, he was the one who had put all the video clips together. And everyone was more than happy to participate!

Side note: Sometimes, you must ask for the things people may not have thought out but that you need. My guess is, like with my friends and husband, they'll love to be a part of something special.

Showered by Love

Besides having that video, I was also showered with love. Literally . . . I had three baby showers. I know it sounds like a bit much, but let me break them down: the one in London in person, the one with friends on Zoom, and the one with family on Zoom. London was the first one, which I hosted for myself. Yup, you heard that right. I hosted one of my own baby showers. I did this for a few reasons. One of them was because I was able to use the church I worked for since we couldn't host it at someone else's home because of, well, COVID. Second, for many of my London friends, it was the first time they'd ever attended a baby shower. They had no idea what to do. They were so excited to attend mine. I learned it's more of an American and African event than a European one. We played baby charades, which was hilarious—watching my friends act out going into labor, breastfeeding, or putting on a diaper. I cried from the laughter. It was one of the few times in my pregnancy when I forgot we were living in a pandemic.

My friend Bethany hosted the next baby shower. She did such a beautiful job. She got photos from my mom and Rafe's mom of the two of us when we were babies and put them in a video. She also interviewed both of them and asked them questions, and then everyone at the shower had to guess if the answer was Rafe or me. For example: Who was so fair with transparent-blond hair that their mom thought the nurses had switched babies by accident, even when her husband assured her that he hadn't left their baby for a minute?

Any guesses? It was me! It has always been my mom's favorite story to tell about me. Bethany ended my baby shower by asking me what I was excited about and nervous about. After I shared how nervous I was about giving birth, my friends prayed for me, and it was a special time for all of us.

My last shower was my family shower. Having my family in the States and Rafe's family spread out between Zimbabwe, Australia, and South Africa was hard. I want to give a shout-out to Auntie Ferne, who woke up at 3:00 a.m. to attend!

Our sisters hosted the shower on Zoom and did such a good job! One of the games we played was "Terminology." For example: What is a *nappy*? That went out to the Americans since it's a word for *diaper* in other parts of the world. What is another word for *stroller*? That was for the non-Americans, and the answer is a *pushchair* or *pram*.

The next game was having everyone guess what we were going to name our baby and the baby's weight, height, due date, whether baby would have hair or no hair, and if so, the hair color. I'll never forget that my Aunt Mary Lou guessed "Wolfgang" for a name. I mean, my family knew I wanted a unique name, but *Wolfgang*? That made us all laugh.

I loved spending time with everyone at my baby showers, and they were such a blessing where I felt loved and supported. But to be honest, they were also bittersweet. None of my family lived near us anymore, and neither did many of our friends. Amid love and joy came sorrow. It was interesting . . . how I could experience so many emotions in one moment.

Distance can make us sink into the depths of despair or fight to keep our heads above water. I chose to fight, especially since we had moved to a new city, and I knew I needed people there to go on walks with and be friends with. I had to build new and great relationships.

Another hard part was that a lot of my friends back home (almost all of my bridesmaids) had already had babies or were pregnant. It was tough to swallow when I didn't get to go through that season with them. These were friends I'd known for over twenty years. Instead of focusing on that, though, Rafe and I decided to sign up for NCT—which, again, stands for National Childbirth Trust.

National Childbirth Trust

Almost everyone in the UK registers in this network. You input your postal code into the system, and it places you in a group and a class with people whose due dates are around the same time as you. You meet people who live nearby and you all learn about the "baby stuff." The class taught us how to have a positive birth experience, how to care for our new babies, including feeding; how to take care of our mental health, and how to find support when needed. It was all great information, but I think a lot of us participated to meet other first-time parents.

I am so thankful for the mommas I met in NCT. For the times they checked in on me, the birthday cards they mailed to me when I barely knew them, the prayers sent via voice notes, the presents dropped off at my door when my grandma passed away, and the dairy-free brownies mailed to me when we were first battling eczema. These women will be women I remember and cherish for the rest of my life. This group surrounded me in a season when I could have been alone. It wasn't who I expected to be my support system, but I'm so thankful they were . . . and still are.

Tips on Ways to Be Supported
(Don't be afraid to share this with friends who don't yet have babies. They just don't know.)

1. Food . . . always food. I was exhausted and sleep-deprived. Thankfully, my mom stocked our freezer—and not just for dinner, but with breakfast burritos. The times I didn't want to cook most were in the mornings.
2. Food again. This time for unlikely situations. We had to go to the emergency room when Zeik's skin got really bad. Alexis (a fellow NCT mom) asked if she could drop off some food when we got home. It was such an incredible gesture and super helpful.
3. Yes, for the third time, *food*. If you're international, you can send friends a link for a food delivery service.
4. New moms may not be ready for you to take their babies out (even for just a walk). So offer to come over to watch the baby while they nap. Or just come over to do their dishes or laundry.

Prayer

God, thank You that You are a God of relationships, a God that brings people into our lives exactly when we need them most. I pray for those searching for a community—that You guide them to one. That You make them brave to share their needs. That they make new friends who are in the same season of life as they are. Who are like-minded and like-hearted. Friends they can lean on when they don't feel like they can stand. Friends that will lift them up and help them battle any lies that try to come into their minds. Friends of different generations that have gone before them. Lord, thank You for sisterhood, and we pray that You continue to bring us together for Your glory. Amen.

CHAPTER SEVEN

Welcome to the World

THE HOSPITAL AND AN EMERGENCY C-SECTION

———

Rafe and I with baby on board reached the end of the third trimester, and I felt ready to *pop*. Besides wanting this baby to be born, I longed for my mom. We went back and forth about when it would be a good time for her to visit Scotland.

Everyone is different. Some people want their moms/parent figures with them; others just want to be with their baby and husband for the first couple of weeks. My mom suggested that she come after Christmas so that we could have our space. I cried out, "No! I need you here!" and I had the feeling the UK government was going to head into a strict lockdown around Christmas time. Thankfully, my mom agreed and arrived a few days before my water broke. It was nice having those few days together with her being able to see me pregnant. We ordered last-minute things that she thought we might need, rearranged our kitchen cupboards, and bought lots of food to make enchiladas and lasagna to store in our freezer. While eating my mom's comfort food and watching cooking shows together, I started to relax. Having her there was most helpful when I would cry, thinking that I was going to be pregnant forever. Here was how those conversations went:

Me: "I think I'm going to be pregnant forever!"
[Tears streaming down my face.]
Mom: "Good thing that's not possible. He'll come."
Me: "No, I might be the one person whose baby just never comes out!"

I've shared that dramatic conversation with many friends who have gone past their due dates as well. The point is to get them to laugh, but also to show them that it's okay if their emotions are all over the place. Or if their thinking is a little irrational. Everyone gets through this!

On November 30, 2020, around noon, I was sitting on the couch knitting a cat for my niece, Addison. Knitting was one of the new lockdown skills I had taught myself. I felt something wet, so I headed up to the bathroom. I wasn't really thinking, just doing. I changed my underwear, put on a pad, and continued knitting. Within an hour or so, I told my mom and Rafe that I was having cramps. They felt like period cramps. My mom said, "You're in labor!" I don't know how I had missed that my water broke!

We continued to watch TV until the contractions started to worsen. My mom suggested I start my breathing exercises. I laughed and told her I didn't have any. I'll never forget what she said: "Well, you better go online and learn some!" So I found a labor breathing video and started putting it into practice. And my goodness, did it help!

After a while, the contractions grew stronger, and at around 7:00 p.m., I was on our staircase, bent over and timing my contractions on an app. At 8:00 p.m., we called the hospital and told them how far apart the contractions were, and they said to head on in. Rafe and I jumped (okay, I waddled) into the car, my mom kissed me on the cheek, and off we went. Driving on a Monday night in Edinburgh during a pandemic, there was no traffic at all. It was the smoothest ride to the hospital ever, and I breathed out gratitude. Rafe was driving, and when I was between contractions, I let our family and friends know we were on our way to the hospital through the group messaging we had set up. I told everyone that Rafe would give updates when he could.

When we arrived, Rafe dropped me off at the birth center and left to park the car. He wasn't allowed inside until there was a room ready for us. I had the waiting room all to myself as the midwife prepared our room.

I thought the birth center was going to be different than a usual hospital waiting room. It was the same. It felt cold and smelled like sanitizer. The midwife was quite the opposite. She seemed warm, gentle, and kind—someone I would grab coffee with but maybe not someone to deliver my child, as she didn't look like she was old enough to do so.

Finally, she let me know I could tell Rafe to come in. And he did, bringing with him a small suitcase and a backpack. As we headed back, I asked the midwife if it looked like we brought too much. She kindly smiled and said most first-time parents do. We made it to our lovely room where I saw a huge bed and a birthing pool.

Once I was settled, the midwife counted the time between my contractions and relayed the information to the senior midwife. When she came back in, she said that they thought I should head home and continue contracting there, emphasizing that it would be more comfortable for me to do at home. Well, that was the last thing I wanted to do—to drive all the way back home!

I let her know I was positive for Strep B and had been told that once my water broke, I would need to be put on antibiotics. The senior midwife then agreed that I should stay, and I was hooked up to an IV in my right arm. It was so uncomfortable. It took the midwife a couple of times to get it in properly, and I thought it might be because she was still a student.

My contractions were getting stronger, so the midwife checked to see how dilated I had become. "Things are progressing quickly," she told us, so I decided to go into the tub to see what it was like to labor in water. I found it more comfortable aside from the fact I couldn't let my IV get in the water. Bless Rafe; he held my arm up for hours so it wouldn't get wet.

Despite the IV placement issues, my midwife was incredible. She loved the worship music we were playing and was so gentle. Throughout my contractions, she would tell me "well done" and cheer me on. Rafe, on the other hand, said, "Good job!" In my angst, I responded, "How do you know if I'm doing a good job?!" For some reason, the phrase *good job* really frustrated me. I advised him he could say whatever the midwife was saying. *Well done.*

As the pain of the contractions grew stronger, I wanted to try a technique called gas and air. Here's the UK's National Health Services' explanation: "it's a mixture of oxygen and nitrous oxide gas. You breathe it in through a mask or mouthpiece that you hold yourself. Gas and air won't remove all the pain, but it can help by reducing it and making it easier to bear. Many women like it because it's easy to use and you control it yourself . . . The gas takes about 15-20 seconds to work, so you breathe it in just as a contraction begins."

Many friends had told me it was helpful during their labor. *Welp*, it made me throw up. After that, I found sitting on the toilet quite comfortable during contractions.

I just wish the bathroom hadn't been so bright. Then, I went and laid on the bed, but the lady in the room next to me started screaming—screaming to the point where I feel like I might have landed in a haunted house rather than a birthing center. My lovely, relaxing room turned into a painful, throwing-up, screaming nightmare. I made the call for an epidural to get out of there as quickly as possible.

The midwife grabbed a wheelchair and took us up to the labor ward. The worst part was having to wear a mask from one room to the other. Having contractions while breathing through a mask was difficult. At this point, it was just before five o'clock in the morning.

We arrived in the room and were introduced to our new midwives. One of them asked how long we'd been living on the street we lived on. We told her for only a couple of months, and she responded with, "My in-laws live a few houses down." What were the chances of that? Then the anesthesiologist who was going to administer the epidural came into the room. He let us know the risks and had me sign a waiver. I didn't know it at the time, but apparently, Rafe was worried and stressed about the side effects.

They sat me up and put my legs over the side of the bed. I arched my back into a c shape and bent over as far as I could. Then I tucked my chin in and did not move. It was possibly the *most* uncomfortable position I've ever been in. The anesthesiologist then told me

I needed to let him know when I was about to have a contraction because I had to be still for the epidural. With each contraction I had, my entire body shook. With my right hand, I held on to Rafe, and in my left, I had another young student midwife's hand. I told her I wouldn't squeeze tightly, but I needed to hold onto her. She smiled.

Finally, a few contractions later, he got the epidural in. Thankfully, Rafe didn't pass out at the sight of the needle. But he told me later that he almost did—he also hadn't eaten in hours, which didn't help! One thing no one told me was that once you get an epidural, it doesn't just take the pain away instantly. It takes about fifteen to twenty minutes to take effect, which feels a lot longer when you're in labor. As it started to kick in, the contractions lessened to what felt like period cramps. Although I couldn't move my legs, I felt more comfortable.

As time went on, our midwives headed out to eat breakfast. A new midwife came in to watch my monitor. She noticed that Zeik's heart rate was dropping and not recovering. So she brought in another midwife, and they started to put my body in different positions to see if that would help. It didn't. Then, the midwife called for the doctor to come in to check what was happening. Surprisingly, I was still feeling calm. I don't know if it was the epidural or the fact that I fully trusted God and the doctors. It was all out of my control, and I let it be.

The doctor decided to check how dilated I had

become, and she was not gentle at all! I looked at my new midwife and told her how painful it felt. She whispered, "I'll make sure she is gentle next time." The doctor informed us that I was eight centimeters dilated and asked if she could scrape the baby's head to get a blood sample to see how much air was in his blood. At first, that sounded alarming. I didn't want them to scratch his head, but at the same time, I knew this would help give me the option to wait a little longer. So I agreed to allow it.

About twenty minutes later, the medical team noticed that Zeik's heart rate was dropping more and recovering less, so the doctor came back in. She looked at me and said, "It's time to go to the theater. If you make it to ten centimeters by then, we will deliver with assistance, but if not, then we'll need to perform a C-section. Is that okay?" This annoyed me, that she asked as if there was any other choice. I said yes. "Okay then, your husband is going to be taken to get scrubs on, and I'm going to press this red button. This red button means that a lot of people are going to enter this room quickly. Everyone has a job, so don't worry." This really calmed me down. I liked knowing that the people coming in were all assigned to their positions and knew what to do. I pretended it was a soccer game. We'd been practicing, and now, it was go time—ready for Friday Night Lights!

The doctor pressed the red button, and they rushed

in, doing whatever they were meant to do, and then wheeled me to the theater. As we got to the surgical suite, I was lifted onto a table where I felt like I was slowly falling off. Everyone in the room introduced themselves and told me what their job was, which, again, was very comforting.

From this experience, I've learned not to make small talk while I'm basically naked under blazing lights. I told one of the doctors on my left that I liked his tattoos, and he responded that he liked mine too. I thought, *How can he see them all?* No one sees them unless I'm wearing a bikini. Then I realized: "Ah, ya. I'm naked." So awkward.

Rafe walked into the room, dressed in the hospital's finest, and I held his hand as he sat next to me. I shared that I was nervous.

"Everything is going to be okay."

On my right side was good ole Ed. Ed was the anesthesiologist administering my pain medication. He told me he was going to spray cold air on my legs and stomach to see if I felt anything. When he did, I was unsure, so I asked if he could do it again. He replied, "As many times as you like."

After that, I confided to Ed: "Sooooo, I want to know what's happening, but at the same time, I don't want to know what's happening."

He grinned. "Sounds good."

The doctor behind the sheet spoke next: "I'm going to

touch you right here, and you tell me if you feel any pain."

"Nope," I replied after the test. Ed turned and looked at me.

"If you did, it would have hurt really bad." I was very thankful for Ed. It seemed as if only minutes went by while I felt the tugging and pulling on my numb body. Then I heard and saw my little boy above the sheet. Zeik had made his way into the world. They asked Rafe if he wanted to cut the cord. "I don't know . . ." He looked toward me.

"It's in the birth plan," I mentioned, so they handed him the scissors. He made sure *not* to look and then cut the cord. In a matter of seconds, they handed a freed Zeik to him. This is the one thing I look back on that makes me sad. I saw Zeik, and then they took him away for a couple of minutes. I thought I'd be the first one to hold him and pull him against my chest. But that's okay, because as I lay on the table, I looked over at Rafe, holding our son, crying with joy. Seeing the love in his eyes made me tear up—a love for our son.

I didn't cry much because I was beyond exhaustion; I was just relieved he was out safely. I feel like there is this pressure to have some emotional response when you see your baby for the first time, and I didn't have it. I didn't experience what I'd seen in videos or movies. Later on, I called my sister and asked her if that was normal.

"Of course! You've known this baby for months since he's been growing inside you, and it was Rafe's first time experiencing him fully." This really made me feel better.

So if you end up having your baby and it's not what you expect it to be, that's okay. We're all different. I've fallen more in love with our boy with each day that has gone by.

Next, I heard, "Do you want to try to stitch her up?"

The student responded, "Really? Yes, I'd love to."

I tried to whisper with the little energy I had. "Rafe, Rafe, did you hear that?" Then, I just gave up. In the end, the doctor said she did a good job. Once they finished, we were wheeled off into another room, and I thanked everyone as we left.

Two new nurses greeted me and attempted to put an IV in my hand but couldn't after stabbing me about four times. "Oh, you have rolling veins!"

"Mmm, I've never had any issues with *that* before in my life." So they ended up finding a doctor who did it in seconds. We asked the staff about different procedures that we thought were common at the hospital. They looked at me as if I was the worst person in the world. Shocked, they told me that it is Zeik's body, therefore, his choice. The staff didn't even know where we could get certain procedures done. Another lesson learned: the UK had different practices than the US and Africa.

I was wheeled to the hallway, which is where we had to say goodbye to Rafe. He kissed Zeik and me and said, "I'll see you soon." He checked that I had everything I needed; then they wheeled me into the elevator, taking me to where I'd spend my first three days healing and learning with Zeik.

Prayer

I pray for those who feel anxious that things might not go their way. For circumstances that we cannot control. May You give us strength to set our minds on You. May You send unexpected people to give us comfort. Keep our eyes open to the blessings that surround us. Amid the unknown, may we feel fully known by our loving Father. Amen.

CHAPTER EIGHT

Bedside Angel

THE LABOR WARD AND A GLIMPSE INTO RECOVERY

———

As I rolled into the room where I'd be staying the next few nights, I was surrounded by curtains. It was still too early for the sun. Scottish winters are quite brutal, particularly with how long the darkness stays. I wondered who might be in the beds that surrounded me, feeling curious about their stories and how their children's births went. Mostly, it was just nice to be by other new moms that had been through what I had just endured. I knew theirs may have been different stories than mine, but we were in it together.

Since I couldn't sit up to get Zeik into his bed, I just laid him next to me. He slept cuddled up to me. I had a button to push whenever I needed help, and I went in and out of sleep—still on pain relievers and exhausted from the day before. As the sun's rays started to peek into the room, an elderly midwife walked in and asked if I'd like some tea and toast. "Yes!" I said happily. I was more conscious of my surroundings and excited to have my first cuppa with my baby.

Soon after, another midwife came in to check on me and talk to me about my medication routine and how they would taper me off of the stronger medication.

A few hours later, in the center of the room, the midwives were mumbling about something. Suddenly, one loudly said, "I can't believe they changed it!" A few seemed happy and others looked frustrated. I wasn't sure what they were talking about, but I was hoping it was about the visiting hours. Because of COVID over the past few months, they had suspended all visiting hours. This had been devastating to me as a first-time mom when all I wanted to do was share every moment of Zeik's first days of life with Rafe. I desperately wanted to be home with Rafe and my mom, but I knew I wasn't ready for that either.

A midwife strode from bed to bed with a huge smile on her face. She was obviously relishing in being the one that delivered the news; one of the other midwives stormed off. The happy midwife got to the end of my bed. "They're opening the visiting hours from 1:00 to 4:00 p.m. today!" What an answer to prayer! I had specifically asked my friends to pray for this very miracle! I called Rafe, and he was thrilled to come and hold our boy again. Only one visitor was allowed, but my mom understood, of course.

Being reunited with Rafe was incredible. To all be together filled my heart with joy and helped put my body at ease. We were thankful for the time we had together bonding as a family of three. I focused on the positives, knowing not all new moms had this opportunity during the lockdown.

When Rafe had to leave, I just wanted to hold on. I didn't want him to let go of my hand. He stayed until the very last minute. Seeing him was the strength I needed to get through another night alone. It gave me a reminder that I was not helpless and that I had support. Being too weak to pick up my son on my own broke my heart, but Rafe's visit was a reminder that I was not helpless and that I had support.

As nighttime began again, so did the shift change for the midwives. I'm pretty sure God sent me an angel on this second night. Thinking about it now, she looked like my sister—a wee bit taller than me, with brown hair and reassuring eyes. She approached me and said, "Okay, I've looked over your chart, and it's time for you to walk." I told her I was scared and didn't know if I could do it. She looked at me and calmly said, "I'll be with you; you can hold onto me." The look in her eyes brought me peace, and I felt like she truly cared about me. That this wasn't just a job to her, and she really wanted to help me heal. As I slid off the bed and stood on my feet, I put one arm around her and slowly walked to the bathroom as blood ran down my leg and trailed behind us. I looked back and my heart sank in my chest; I didn't know if this amount of blood was normal or not. It was as if she knew what I was thinking.

"It's a blood clot, and it's good it's come out." She opened the door and helped sit me down in a chair in front of the shower. She assured me that she'd keep an eye on Zeik, and if I needed anything, to just say so. Having warm water rush down my sore body felt like a dream, like I was in a day spa in the Maldives. Washing my hair made me feel brand new. Afterward, I attempted to walk to the toilet by myself, which was difficult. I don't need to go into details there, but blood was still gushing out and all pooling around the floor. My midwife arrived and told me not to worry, that she'd hose it all down the drain. I dried off and got dressed, and then she helped me make my way back to the bed.

I never thought going to the bathroom and taking a shower would be such victories. It was the start of me learning how to appreciate those little victories. To really celebrate small accomplishments. The struggle helped me learn to be patient with my body. Although I must say, I did miss the catheter; it was quite convenient to not have to get up and go to the bathroom. *Just sayin'.*

Shift Change

The next night, my angel didn't come back. Instead, I was assigned the grumpiest woman ever. She got mad at me because I couldn't change my baby's diaper. I mean, I couldn't even lift him up myself. What did she expect? I knew I had to let her attitude go; maybe something else was going on in her life. But she didn't need to throw Zeik's outfit at me after she changed him for me to put it on. But I was too exhausted to be mad.

Whenever the baby behind the curtain next to us cried, it would get Zeik going. It was as if they had planned to take turns, which I joked about with the baby's mom. I couldn't see her, but I heard her laugh.

We made it through the night, and the next day, she hobbled over to a chair by my bed and we chatted for a bit. She was a petite woman with long black hair, seemingly from the Middle East. She told me about each mother in the room. One mom's baby had a bad case of jaundice; another she didn't know about because the mom kept her curtains closed the whole time. We shared our birth stories and sadly, she had lost a lot of blood. It had been a difficult recovery since her baby was tired and struggling to breastfeed. If there had been a sign outside our room, I feel like it would say "Births didn't go as planned." All of us were going through something. She reminded me of that. I wish I had gotten her name, but I'll never forget the kindness she showed me—and the excitement we both shared when we were released to go home on the same day.

Homebound

Rafe came into the hospital to take Zeik and me home as my mom waited in the car . . . for hours. It took longer to get checked out than expected. I asked if I could take some more pads and hospital underwear home. Apparently, they are way better than any brand you can buy—so said the moms from my baby group. I also took the blanket they wrapped Zeik in. After all, they didn't say I couldn't! Then we went through the medication protocol with the midwife. She showed Rafe how to administer a shot in my thigh.

Yup, you heard that correctly. For the next ten days, Rafe had to put a shot in my thigh, switching from left to right each day. They said it was to prevent blood clots. When I told my sister about it, she said they don't do that in America. *Great*, I thought. I'm so terrible with needles.

We dressed Zeik in a cute outfit, took his photo with our polaroid camera, and off we went. I was so happy to see my mom again and have her meet Zeik. The ride home felt like the Indiana Jones ride at Disneyland. If you've never been on that, know this: it's bumpy. I felt every bump, rock, and groove on the road, and it hurt my incision to even sit up in the car for that long.

Rafe and my mom helped Zeik and me into the house and up the stairs. I crawled into bed, thankful to my husband for changing all of the sheets. Who doesn't love a freshly changed bed? Then we all sat around adoring Zeik.

A few hours later, our baby son was inconsolable. I thought, *Wow, is this what it's going to be like?* My mom heard the commotion and came upstairs. She told us to give him the dummy. "No, they said not to!"

"Just do it," she said. In desperation for the screaming to stop, we put the dummy in his mouth and, like magic, it worked.

When our health visitor came, she noticed that Zeik had lost quite a bit of weight. It was taking a long time for my breastmilk to come in, and his poop wasn't looking right.

*Side note: Get ready, soon-to-be moms. You're about to have a lot of poop photos on your phone.

The health visitor also let us know that Zeik was dehydrated. We ended up topping him off with formula, and he was finally settling more and more. Though he still loved his pacifier, he was not needing it like he had been.

Something my mom taught me was that I needed to be patient with Rafe. She reminded me that as moms, we have these natural instincts. We just seem to know what to do. Dads don't necessarily have this innate knowledge. So I allowed Rafe to learn and gave him space to do so. I vowed to be kind to him as he did the best he could. I needed to hear this since I was getting so frustrated with him—frustrated with the little things, like how long the man took to change a nappy! It sounds silly, but it took him forever. Rafe would sing to Zeik as he changed each one. I decided to take my mom's advice and just let him do things his way. What worked for him and Zeik was different from Zeik's and my routine.

One time, my mom was sitting on the side of my bed and smiled as we listened to Rafe sing, "Dad's changing your nappy; Dad's changing your nappy." Then, he suddenly started singing "Ohhhh dear, ohhhh dear, you're peeing on your dad. Ohhhhh dear." My mom and I laughed and laughed.

As the days went by, they were filled with watching cooking shows, learning how to find a new life routine, eating my mom's comfort food, having her rub my legs, enjoying Zeik's every movement, and trying not to laugh because it hurt my incision—and boy, was that hard to do. I'll never forget when Rafe made fruit bowls for my mom and me. It was so sweet of him. He even added a little bit of yogurt on top. As we took our first bites, we noticed they tasted like onion. My mom and I both made odd faces. I loudly asked, "Raaaaffee, were there onions by the apples?"

"Yeah."

I *thought* the apples had tasted funny. My mom and I burst out laughing. I told her she needed to leave the room because we couldn't even look at each other without laughing. It hurt so bad, but it was nice to have that kind of joy again. The kind of happiness where you laugh so hard you can barely talk about it.

Over the next few days, my mom made us enchiladas, breakfast burritos, and lasagna, storing it all in our freezing downstairs. It lasted us for a few months. Later, when we ate the meals, it made me feel like she was still with us. Her being there helped us grow closer than ever before. I needed my mom in those days, and I'm so thankful we got to share Zeik's first few weeks of life with her. It made me realize: *Wow, I'm a mom, too.* The same love I have for mine, the same comfort she brings me, I bring to my son. He needs me. This really made me wish my mom lived closer.

The morning she left, I couldn't help but cry. I didn't know the next time we'd see her. She told me not to get upset, that she'd see me soon, and hugged me good-bye. I went to the window, crying as I watched her car drive away. Her leaving made me feel more helpless. I couldn't get out of my bed alone, sit up alone, or really do anything alone. It had been wonderful to have my mom there to ask for help so I didn't feel like I was putting it all on Rafe.

Sealed, but not Healed

A new midwife came to take out my stitches when my regular one was on holiday. The new midwife was an absolute joy and brought so much energy into the house. I was scared to get my stitches taken out, afraid suddenly everything was going to fall out of me. A bit dramatic, I know, but I imagined it! She started to remove them, and it didn't sting until the very end. She said usually one side is sorer because they pull on one more than the other during the surgery. Not sure how I felt about that last bit of information, but at least it made sense. I remembered them tugging on my right side more. It was such a blessing to have them removed at home in my bed.

I asked the midwife how my scar looked. She said it looked good, and that I should know I'm "sealed, but not healed." At that moment, I felt a profound peace sweep over me. The words sunk deep into my soul. When she left, I grabbed my phone, opened my notes, and typed "Sealed, not healed." I sat in awe of those three words. I didn't know what I was going to do with them, but I believed they were leading me to something. I prayed in the shower, asking God, "What now? What do they mean? What am I supposed to do?" I heard in my spirit Him saying, "Wait. You just became a mom. Let's focus on that first."

What Now?

As the days went on, I think I showered more than any person ever. The warm water felt healing to my body. Plus, no one had told me about night sweats after birth. That's how your body gets rid of the extra fluid. It was like I was sleeping in a swamp, and when I would wake up, I'd be drenched.

Taking shower after shower, I believe, caused the next difficulty—an ear infection. I had never had one as an adult. It was one of the most painful things I'd ever been through. I even thought I would rather go through contractions again. With those, at least you know you're getting a baby. With an ear infection, there is no reward at the end. The sharp pain would cause me to cry through the night, and it took weeks to figure out the correct medication, mainly since doctors were only taking calls; no one would see me in person.

When I would manage to actually get some sleep, I'd have the worst nightmares. They were always about Rafe leaving me and me running after him to come back. He'd get in a car, and I'd watch him as he drove away. Or there were other dreams of me telling him he wasn't the father. I would wake up clinging to him because they felt so real. I relentlessly prayed for these nightmares to go away. They started to ease when I was just about off all of my medication. I was thankful for the meds, but perhaps more so for the dreams to stop.

I wasn't the only one experiencing bad dreams. Rafe would wake me up in the middle of the night searching through the bed. I'd ask him what he was doing, and he'd yell that Zeik was stuck in the duvet! Rafe had many recurring dreams that our son had somehow managed to get stuck in our sheets. I had to remind him that everything was okay, that Zeik was asleep in the side cot.

A couple of months went by, and these three words popped up in my head again: sealed, not healed. I thought, "Okay, God, do you want me to start a podcast, write a book, maintain a YouTube channel? What do I do with these words?" When the idea of a book surfaced, I was intrigued. But writing about my birth story felt odd to me. I hadn't even filled out those week-to-week baby books. I'm also not one of those people who is super passionate about birth. We all know someone who is, and hey, I'm thankful for them, but I'm just not one of them. So I prayed.

"God, if you want me to write a book, well then, have two other people tell me." I was looking for confirmation. The next day, I received a random message from a lady I had gone to church with back home in the States. After messaging back and forth, I told her I was thinking about writing a book. She responded with, "*A book!* That is incredible! When I was sending you the previous message, I was honestly going to say, 'Have you ever thought about writing a book?'"

I was a wee bit skeptical. But I still took that as person number one. A couple of days later, we were on the phone with Rafe's auntie, and after I said something, she responded, "You should put that in your book!" She had no idea I was thinking about writing a book; I didn't even bring it up on the call. My mouth dropped and Rafe chuckled. *Okay, God, I hear you. I'll write this book.* So here we are. You've made it this far into reading about my birth story with Zeik. I hope you're still enjoying it or starting to feel like we're friends. I hope it reminds you of things God has told you to do that you haven't started yet. Go for it, don't wait for tomorrow. Sometimes the only person that stops you is you.

Prayer

God, how exciting that we get to partner with You. That You have placed specific desires in our heart that bring us joy. That all You ask us to do is say yes and be disciplined to do what is asked. God, I pray for those who are in the waiting, who are unsure of how to begin. I pray You bring clarity to their minds. Remind them that if it is from You, it is good, and that all things are possible in Your will. I thank you, Lord, that You invite Your children to be part of something bigger than themselves. God, pour in fresh ideas and thoughts and give us Your loving guidance. Amen.

CHAPTER NINE

Faith That Heals

JESUS MEETS US WHERE WE'RE AT

———

We can't move on in the story without diving into healing. I spoke on Mark 5:21–34 (TPT) during the lockdown. I inserted the Scripture below for you to read before we break it down together.

> After Jesus returned from across the lake, a
> huge crowd of people quickly gathered around
> him on the shoreline. Just then, a man saw that it
> was Jesus, so he pushed through the crowd and
> threw himself down at his feet. His name was
> Jairus, a Jewish official who was in charge of the
> synagogue. He pleaded with Jesus, saying over

and over, "Please come with me! My little daughter is at the point of death, and she's only twelve years old! Come and lay your hands on her and heal her and she will live!"

Immediately Jesus went with him, and the huge crowd followed, pressing in on him from all sides.

Now, in the crowd that day was a woman who had suffered horribly from continual bleeding for twelve years. She had endured a great deal under the care of various doctors, yet in spite of spending all she had on their treatments, she was getting worse instead of better. When she heard about Jesus' healing power, she pushed through the crowd and came up from behind him and touched his prayer shawl. For she kept saying to herself, "If I could touch even his clothes, I know I will be healed." As soon as her hand touched him, her bleeding immediately stopped! She knew it, for she could feel her body instantly being healed of her disease!

Jesus knew at once that someone had touched him, for he felt the power that always surged around him had passed through him for someone to be healed. He turned and spoke to the crowd, saying, "Who touched my clothes?" His disciples answered, "What do you mean, who touched you? Look at this huge crowd—

they're all pressing up against you." But Jesus'
eyes swept across the crowd, looking for the
one who had touched him for healing.
When the woman who experienced this mir-
acle realized what had happened to her, she
came before him, trembling with fear, and threw
herself down at his feet, saying, "I was the one
who touched you." And she told him her story of
what had just happened.

Then Jesus said to her, "Daughter, because
you dared to believe, your faith has healed you.
Go with peace in your heart, and be free from
your suffering!"

The way I read Scripture is to place myself in the
setting as if I'm there. Let's do this! Jesus was approaching the shore on a fisherman's boat. It had been a long
journey, so I'm sure he was tired—as were the disciples.
They all probably smelled like fish. As they docked,
one of the synagogue leaders rushed to Jesus. Now,
this wasn't just anyone. This religious leader was well
known, in high standing, and a pillar of the community.
He suddenly dropped to his knees in utter desperation.
He was seeking out Jesus to heal his daughter because
she was dying. He pleaded for Jesus to come and visit
his home to heal her. I'm sure if I was in his situation,
I'd push through the crowd too. Jesus agreed to follow
him. He didn't take a water break or stop for food; he

just went. Oh, how I'd probably just want to sit on the ground for a little bit and rest after the long day that Jesus had had.

As they walked along the road, a large crowd followed them, pressing tightly against Jesus. Everyone was touching everyone, trying to get closer to the Rabbi. The story then turns its focus to a woman in the crowd. She had been bleeding for twelve years. *Twelve years.* I don't even like getting my period once a month. She had tried everything this world has to offer. I imagine she spent all of her money on doctors with nothing to show for it. No cure, nothing that helped—she just got continually worse. When you were bleeding like that in those days, you couldn't go anywhere. This woman would have been a complete outcast of the community, isolated from everyone around her, presumably with no money, and just trying to survive.

But she did have something. She had faith that if she could just touch Jesus, she'd be healed. That's all she needed—one touch. One moment, and she'd be restored. What an incredible faith that is.

Spoiler alert: As she touched Jesus's clothes, the bleeding stopped, and her body was freed.

Now, this is one of the best parts of the story, in my opinion. Jesus turned around and asked who had touched him. The disciples likely thought, "Uh, Jesus, everyone is touching you; come on now." Jesus didn't just ask who touched his clothes because he couldn't figure out who it was. He asked because he wanted to first restore the woman's name. She would no longer be an outcast; she was now called a daughter. Just like you are. He wanted people to see her, to see she was redeemed. He also wanted her to be bold and testify by stepping forward, and to see that when she approached him, she didn't need to tremble. He listened to everything she had to say, and he made her feel not only known but also heard. Because of Jesus she was able to now live in peace.

If we rewind a little bit, I often think of Jairus, the synagogue leader, as all this went down. After all, they were on their way to heal his dying daughter, and Jesus stopped for this woman. If I was Jairus, I'd be tapping my foot like, *Come on, Jesus; we got to go!* That's the thing: God's timing for healing . . . it looks different from ours. We don't always know his plan or how it will all play out. No matter how desperate our situations, no matter how difficult things are for us—or for our families—we are never out of His reach. Restoration and healing first come from believing in Him and becoming a son or daughter in Christ.

I don't know what stood out to you most in this story. To me, it's about two people who were in utter need of Jesus, and He met them exactly where they were. How beautiful! My pregnancy wasn't easy, and healing from my C-section was painful, but the peace Jesus brought me through it all transcended all of that. He is with you,

He is for you, He wants to hear all about it, and He calls you daughter.

Soon, you will meet your child (or maybe you have already). Once you do, you'll come to realize the word *daughter* or *son* has a stronger meaning after you become a mom. The word becomes precious and so intimate. There's a sense of belonging when you say it, a sense that a little human belongs to you. I pray that in this time, you feel the same. That you feel known as a daughter by a Father that looks at you with more love than you can imagine.

Prayer

Lord, thank You that You are a God of intimacy. That You are tender and loving. I'm so thankful that no hardship is too difficult for You. I pray for those who are suffering. For those who feel like outcasts and alone in the world. I pray for restoration over our bodies, minds, and souls. I pray that You cleanse us with your goodness. That You refresh every area of our lives. I pray You remind us of who we are in You. I pray You give us patience for the day ahead and moments to pause to lean on You. Amen.

CHAPTER TEN

I'll Always Love You

LOVING FROM GENERATION TO GENERATION

This part of my birth story, in the early days of motherhood, brought the most difficult loss I've ever experienced. It has been hard for me to think about what to share with you. How do I honor the life of my grandma in just one chapter? How do I convey the deep hurt, loss, and disbelief in the fact that she's gone through a simple black-and-white medium? I'll do my best, but I don't think mere words can describe how much I love and miss her.

Around the time Zeik was born, we found out my grandma had suffered a stroke. It was close to the worst news I could get. My mom was very calm about it, as she didn't want to add any extra stress to the first few weeks of me becoming a mother. As time went on, however, my grandma's health kept declining.

My grandma was witty and always spoke her mind. She didn't have a filter, and that's what we loved about her. She was always busy, on the go—attending her Japanese church, getting one of us to take her to Costco to get her dog a hotdog, and always going out to lunch with family. She was very loving in her own way. Not through affection but in prayers. Always asking me how I was and telling me she was praying for me.

Before I had left the States, I asked my sister to promise me that if something happened to grandma, she'd let me know. I didn't want to be kept in the dark. She upheld her promise. I felt deep gratitude and thankfulness for my sister and also deep despair. It broke my heart that I couldn't be there after the stroke, not only for my grandma but for my whole family—for my mom, aunt, and sister. Especially my sister, because she spent many nights sleeping at the hospital with our grandma.

Being away and not seeing my grandma for over a year crushed me. It made me feel like none of the news was real. *How could this be happening? Why now?* I know . . . it's not like there is any good time for a stroke, but my grandma didn't get to see me while I was pregnant, and then, with this news, I had little hope left that she'd be able to meet my son.

I'd go on walks, grappling with wanting to see her

one more time but also not wanting her to be in any pain. My grandma had looked forward to Heaven, waited with patience to be with Jesus, for years. One time, I was visiting her at her house, and she told me the story of how she had fallen off of her chair earlier that day. She said she had laid there, waiting for Jesus to get her, but he never came. She was so mad about it! *Oh, Grandma!* I thought.

She was ready, but none of us were. I would spend hours crying through the night, wanting to jump on a flight and go home. But I couldn't, not with COVID restrictions and a newborn. It was the first time during the pandemic that the sacrifices the world was making and the lack of global mobility really hit me, gutting me to my core. Anger rose in me in the form of tears. I would curl up in a ball on my bed, wanting to shut out the world.

I've tried to recall the last time I saw my grandma, which was on my wedding day, and I don't even remember saying goodbye to her. I don't even remember our last moments together. I feel like I barely saw her because I was so busy. That thought makes me cry every time I have it. It brings me so much guilt and heartache. I just want to go back and give her one more hug. To tell her I love her and have her reply with, "I love you, too, Honey."

One night, I prayed that my grandma would feel like I was there too. That she would know I was with her in spirit. And something astonishing happened. The next day, I called my mom to check in and see how Grandma was doing. She told me that Grandma said she thought I was sitting on the end of her bed. She had even continued talking as if I was there. That meant so much and still breaks me to this day. As hard as it was to learn that she was hallucinating during this time, I felt like it was also an answer to prayer.

Weeks later, I was knitting a scarf. I paused to text a group of friends and ask them to pray for my grandma. But I felt a nudge in my heart that stopped me from messaging them. I decided, *No, this is something I need to do by myself.* I prayed that God would give her peace. I told Him I'd miss her so much and that I wished I could say goodbye, but I knew she was going to where she always wanted to be—Heaven.

Moments later, I got the call that she had passed away. First, I felt a wave of peace. I was thankful that I had just prayed. Then came the sorrow and with it, a flood of tears. Rafe was at the grocery store, so I ran up the stairs, just wanting to be with my baby. I sat in the rocking chair, crying next to his crib as he slept. Zeik brought me comfort. Loving my son so deeply, just as I loved my grandma so deeply, was cathartic. The two together felt like a hug. I felt held.

I wasn't able to attend the memorial because of the pandemic. I won't see her grave for over a year from the day she passed. I still don't know when I'll get to go home. I know she's not there at her gravesite, but I wonder if it would help me process. I don't know. I still can't imagine that she won't be upstairs in her room, watching Japanese soap operas at my Aunt Mary Lou's house. That I won't be taking her out to lunch again. That she won't be there for the holidays. That on every vacation I go on, I won't be bringing something back just for her. I don't know how to process this from across the world.

My sister did an incredible job speaking at my grandma's memorial. She had Wiley, my brother-in-law, set up her phone so I could watch live from Edinburgh. What she said was beautiful. She was composed and loving, and I was so proud of how my sister honored our grandma's life. Sarah asked all the other grandchildren to write about something that Grandma taught us. It made everyone laugh. My grandma taught me that when you go shopping, always dress like you're homeless so no one will help you. *Oh, Grandma.* Since I wasn't there, I wrote my grandma a letter that was in the order of service. Here's what I wrote:

Dear Grandma,

I'm sorry I can't be there today. I'm sorry I couldn't visit in your final year, months, and days. I wish I could hear you say "I love you, Honey" one more time. The day you passed, I almost messaged some friends to say a prayer for you. That thought got interrupted by God

*saying, "No, you pray for her." I prayed you'd
no longer be in pain and that you would be
in peace. That you would feel comforted and
loved. That you knew I was with you in spirit. A
few hours later, I got the call from Mom that you
had passed away. Before the tears, I felt comfort. Comfort knowing that you are home. That
you are with Grandpa and the rest of our family
and your friends. Comfort that you are no longer
in pain. Comfort that you are with Jesus. I didn't
and I still don't want to let you go, but I know
you're where you're meant to be. I know I'll see
you in Heaven one day, and what a glorious day
it will be.*

*In the meantime, I know you're one of the
angels who watch over me. I know you see my
son from Heaven and delight in him. Oh, how I
wish you could be here to hold him and watch
him grow. I can't wait to tell him all about you.
I think you'd be proud of me, Grandma. I'm
becoming the mother I am because of you, my
mom, my aunt, my sister, and all the special
women in our family. Grandma, thank you for
always loving me, laughing with me, and taking
silly photos with me. I'll always cherish our lunch
dates, just you and me. I'm so blessed for all the
joyful memories that surface when I think of you.
I'm so glad that I had so much time with you.*

*It's going to be so hard to come home and
not have you there. When I moved, you said,
"You're just like me"—words I'll forever cling to.
I'm so proud to be your granddaughter and that
you saw yourself in me.*

*I promise to visit your gravesite, as I know
you visited Grandpa's every year. You're in so
many places, Grandma. A piece of you resides
in all of our hearts. I'll always carry you in mine.
This isn't a goodbye; it's an "I'll be seeing you."
I'm so thankful that the last thing I said to you
was "I love you, and I'm praying for you." You
replied, "I love you too, honey. That's all I need."
I love you, Grandma. Life won't be the same
without you.*

Until Heaven,
Caitlyn

Linda Matsue Reed
In Loving Memory,
February 11, 1930 to February 27, 2021

Here are some life lessons from my sister, cousins,
niece, and nephew. I hope you find joy in them or at
least learn a thing or two from my grandma.

• She taught me so much about cooking! How to just

trust yourself in the process, how to enjoy it, how to taste things as you go and make it the way you like it. And that making food for people is an act of love. I'll never forget her making a sandwich for a dog.

• I 100% attribute my love for the PNW [Pacific Northwest] to Grandma. I cannot go to the coast without thinking of her. She taught me about six different solitaire games and how to make gravy and wrap gyoza, and I'll never forget how fun it was to work at the Bento Box with her.

• One lesson Grandma taught me that I relay to all of the children I teach is that when you're washing your hands, make sure you don't forget your thumbs. I think of her so many times a day because of this advice.

• I'd say Grandma taught me the importance of showing up and being there for family. Even if you don't want to listen or, in Grandma's case, you turn off your hearing aids. No matter what, she was always there. Which often mattered more than words.

• Grandma taught me how to always be hardworking. She would encourage me to get a good education. She always supported me in my career choices. She was always my cheerleader in life events.

• She was always there for me—whether it was a sports game or school event, she would always be sure to be there. She taught me the value of commitment and that you have to follow through on things. She always made sure I would get to every practice and wouldn't let me fake being sick to stay home from school. She taught me the value of hard work. During the summers when I was growing up, she would always take me out on trips with her to get supplies for the sushi restaurant, and when I got older, I would help out by bussing tables. I was able to see what it takes to run a business at a very young age.

• My grandma taught me how to sew. I'd get the needle, she'd put the thread in it, and I would go up and down and up and down. Even though my bunny's leg came out a little crooked, it looked perfect to us. I'm also so good at art because my grandma colored with me a lot. We colored and colored and colored; that's why I'm such a good artist.

• Grandma Linda helped me get my helmet on when we went outside. I liked to hold her hand when she came into my house. We went to the store A LOT together, for a REALLY, REALLY long time. I loved her . . . She let me "drive" when mommy was in the store. When mommy came out, she was not happy, and Grandma just laughed. I liked that.

In conclusion, she made an impact. She taught us how to work hard, how to love hard, and how to get up before anyone saw that it hurt. I asked her in the hospital what she wanted me to remember. She said, "Be nice to everybody!"

As people left the service, they were given a daffodil

to plant in memory of her so that year after year, as it grows back, they'll think of her. She loved flowers. She passed away at the end of February, and amazingly, daffodils bloom in the UK in March. I felt her love surround me in this country. She was everywhere I looked in Edinburgh.

God was speaking to me through His Creation. I heard Him whispering, "Enjoy, my child. Delight in this beauty as I delight in all My Creation . . . in you." All of the flowers I saw felt like a gift from Him, reminding me of His love for me, saying, "I see you."

I didn't know then that months later, I would be telling this story to a group of teenagers. I was asked to speak at a Christian Union meeting at a Rugby boarding school. I'd spoken there a few times pre-pandemic and ended up doing a live stream since I no longer lived in London. I was given the prompt *A God Who Speaks* and was asked to use Psalm 19 as a reference.

Psalm 19

The heavens declare the glory of God;
the skies proclaim the work of his hands.
Day after day they pour forth speech;
night after night they reveal knowledge.
They have no speech, they use no words;
no sound is heard from them.
Yet their voice goes out into all the earth,

their words to the ends of the world.
In the heavens God has pitched a tent for the sun.
It is like a bridegroom coming out of his chamber,
like a champion rejoicing to run his course.
It rises at one end of the heavens
and makes its circuit to the other;
nothing is deprived of its warmth.

There are so many voices in this world that are trying to capture our attention. With all of the noise around us, it's hard to tune into God's, or we forget to even try to hear Him. Because of this, it's such a vital thing to learn *how* to hear from Him. It's been an area in my life that has caused insecurity because it's easy to compare yourself to other people who have clearly heard from God. I've thought, *What about me? What are You saying to me, God? What do You want me to do?*

The incredible thing about God is that He wants to speak to His children; He desires a personal, one-on-one relationship with you. He'll speak to you and meet you in ways that are tailored to your heart.

So, how do we hear from Him? In Scripture, we can find many ways to hear from God, such as reading the Bible, appreciating His Creation, worshiping Him, having fellowship with others, and also visions, dreams, passing thoughts, circumstances, and even an audible voice. I have yet to hear an audible voice, but wouldn't that be incredible? "Cait, it's your Father. Don't forget to brush

Zeik's teeth." Seriously, though . . . I keep forgetting to do that.

When reading through Psalm 19, two of the things that come to mind are sunrises and sunsets. The fact that every day, there's a morning and an evening. Every day, God is pursuing us. He is around us all of the time, and there is no one He doesn't want to reach. "Yet, their voice goes out into all the earth, their words to the ends of the world" (verse 4). Can you think of a time when you've been in awe of a sunrise, sunset, beach, or mountain range? Maybe you didn't realize it, but that awe, that wonder, is something God created to speak to you. How vast His love is for you.

I'm glad I had the opportunity to speak about my grandma's passing to a group of teenagers. It was another small way of honoring her life. It was also special in that I'd never really thought much about how God speaks to us through His Creation before speaking on Psalm 19. It's like my grandma and God were teaching me something new from Heaven. As I told the students the story of how I hadn't been able to see my grandma in so long and that I felt like God was gifting me with the daffodils in bloom, I got very emotional. I had to pause to try to not break down in tears. I wanted to be authentic and open with them. To show them that even in one of my darkest times, I had found a joy that could only come from God. I reminded them that hearing from God isn't complicated; it isn't something to overthink, and you don't have to go on some wild adventure or earn the right to speak to Him. Just like my own son doesn't need to do anything to earn my love for him.

At the end of my talk, I prayed for the teenagers and gave them a moment to respond to the message. I asked them to close their eyes and raise their hand if they desired to hear more from God or if they wanted to start on the journey of getting to know who Jesus is. Hands were lifted all over the room for both questions. It brought my heart so much joy—that God used me to talk about Scripture and what He's done in my life.

After the prayer, they opened the floor for the students to ask me questions. I allowed any question they could think of. In the past, there had been some random questions, but tonight, it was different. They asked meaningful questions about what I had just talked about. One that stood out to me the most was from a young man who said, "Well, not all of us have a powerful story like you do. How do we know if God is speaking to us? And how do we know it's not just a coincidence?" I told him I understood what he was saying. I didn't think that, many years before then, God had made sure daffodils would be in bloom just because He knew I would be in the UK and they reminded me of my grandma – although I did tell this young man that I do think God used His Creation to speak to me.

I can tell you about many times in my life where God has spoken to me and the different ways He did. I have story after story. There are also stories in the Bible. All in all, they're just stories. You have to have your own relationship with God to experience how He speaks to you. Then you'll see they're not just coincidences.

Someone once explained having faith to me by pointing to a chair. "Do you think if you sit in that chair over there, it'll hold you up?" I said yes. "How do you know if you don't sit in it? All the screws could be loose, and you could fall." Until you sit in it, until you spend time with God, pursuing Him yourself, you'll never know. My hope for you is that wherever you are in your faith, you will pursue God just as He pursues you every day. That whatever answers you're searching for, you find peace in Him.

Prayer

I pray that God comforts the hearts of those who have lost their loved ones. That He captures our attention through the beauty of His Creation. I pray He catches every tear that falls. I pray He comforts those who are away from family. I pray that no one feels alone and that His love wraps around us all. And that we feel a warmth in our hearts that soothes our souls. It's a love that only You can give, God. Hold us, Lord. Hold us.

CHAPTER ELEVEN

Jesus and Eczema

HOW GOD CARRIED US THROUGH ZEIK'S HEALTH BATTLE

———

The day after my grandma passed away, Rafe brought me breakfast in bed. The winter sun shone through the window, and Rafe turned on the song "Soak Up the Sun" by Sherly Crow. He danced with Zeik in front of the bed. Watching them, I believed everything would be okay.

Then I noticed that Zeik's face was swelling, with patchy redness all over his neck. Panicked, I pointed it out to Rafe, and we rushed to the emergency room. Thankfully, it was only a 15-minute drive. We called ahead, letting them know we were coming. We didn't want to waste any time.

Rafe pulled up and dropped Zeik and me off, and I raced inside. Shortly after, we were seen by the doctor. After looking at Zeik's skin, she said she didn't know what it was. She recommended we wait a few days to see if it passed. She let me know that if I wanted another opinion, I could go to the children's hospital and have them take a look.

Something wasn't sitting right with me, so I told her that I'd like to do just that. Nodding her head in understanding, she called to give me a referral and got us an appointment set for a little later that day.

I walked back to the car holding tightly to Zeik and let Rafe know the plan. During that drive home to wait before the appointment at the children's hospital, I let a few of the moms in my NCT group know what was going on. They knew I had just lost my grandma, and having to go to the A&E/ER with your baby is just plain scary any day.

As we pulled up to the children's hospital at the designated time, the husband of one of the NCT moms was there strolling his baby. He walked us up to the hospital door and reminded us that they lived right down the road if we needed anything. Later, Hannah, his wife, dropped off some chocolate, leaving it on our car window. Little things like that, especially with being new to the city, were a blessing to us.

Rafe and I went inside the hospital and, of course, they let us know that only one of us could be in there.

Rafe headed back outside and waited by our hospital window, eager to hear any news, longing to be with us as he stood in the cold.

Inside the room, it couldn't have been any brighter. I asked if they could turn off the lights so Zeik could sleep. We were both exhausted, and I wanted him to nap when he could. The nurses came in, and I had to remove his clothes so they could measure his true weight. Once they exited the room, we were left to play the hospital waiting game.

Nothing happened as the hours passed. I feel like when you're in the hospital, it's as if time slows down and everything takes forever. My emotions were turning numb, and I was struggling to keep it together. Eventually, the doctor entered our room, wanting to weigh Zeik again, which I thought was odd. I took his clothes off again. He weighed the same amount as the first time. They thought maybe the scale was faulty. Zeik hadn't gained any weight. They were shocked; he had gone from the 91st percentile to the 1st percentile since his birth. The doctor took a look at his skin and told me she thought it was *eczema* and a possible dairy allergy. It was the first time I'd heard that word, eczema. Little did I know then that I would be doing more research about this skin condition than I ever had about anything else in my life.

The doctor wanted to do a blood and urine sample too. I noticed it was getting dark outside, and suddenly,

I felt like I was going to pass out on the floor. I texted Rafe, and we decided to make a switch. I felt guilty leaving Zeik when he was about to have blood taken, but emotionally, I couldn't do it. I knew Rafe was in a better headspace than me. As we switched, I felt judgment seeping from the nurses. The frowns followed me as I walked out the door. I sat in our car and let our family know what was happening.

As I waited, I wished I could be sleeping in our bed, but more than that, I hoped and prayed that our baby would be okay. I also cried, grieving the loss of my grandma.

After another hour went by, I called Rafe to ask him what was going on. "Zeik is doing good, and they gave me a little bucket to catch some urine in." I was outraged that they expected us to wait until he peed. Who knew how long that would take? It was nearly 7:00 p.m. and we were all worn out. I told Rafe to tell the nurse to give him a vial for us to take home, and that we'd bring back a sample the next day, but for now, we were leaving. They obliged. This was the first time I had to advocate for my son. I couldn't have imagined at the time that I'd have to continue to do so in the coming months.

Since Zeik's weight was so low, they assigned us a dietary specialist. She suggested we have Zeik consume a non-dairy formula to see if it would help. Then, over the next few months, they wanted our health visitor to come and weigh him every few weeks.

We started to see his weight come up. In the meantime, I was trying to pump to keep my milk supply up. I wanted to keep breastfeeding, and I gave it a full month until I stopped. I wasn't able to keep my supply up, and I felt like a failure. I believe there is an unspoken pressure—though, sometimes, it is overt and spoken aloud—to breastfeed for as long as possible. Don't get me wrong; it's an incredible experience. And it's so healthy for the baby (and the mom) to do it. But not everyone can. It's tougher for some—like me. I tried, and it was easy in the beginning, but then all of a sudden, it wasn't. I chose my mental health over breastfeeding, and I learned to appreciate that decision. Not feeling like a failure every day was healthier for me and my baby. I want to share this because no matter what your story ends up being with your child, it's your story. These are your choices, and you know what's best. (Also, when they're five years old, running around and heading to school, I'm pretty sure no one is going to say, "Oh, look at that kid over there, he was definitely breast-fed.")

Even though Zeik's weight was coming back up, we still couldn't figure out his skin issue. The doctors advised us to use steroid cream and then wished us luck, hoping he'd grow out of it. To me, it seemed like they were covering up his open wounds with a Band-Aid. It might look better, but long-term steroid use isn't good for a baby. I started to research the effects of steroid cream use and dependency on children. I found that daily use could actually make it worse. I was determined to find another solution.

The Jesus Part

Why did I title this chapter "Jesus and Eczema"? How do these two come together? Well, around Easter of 2021, Zeik had his worst eczema flare-up to date. We were once again back at the A&E/ER because I didn't know what to do. It was impossible to be seen by a general practitioner and we had to do something. The entirety of the backs of Zeik's arms and shoulders were open, seeping wounds. It was horrible. Thankfully, the doctor was so lovely and empathetic toward me. She gave me every cream they had in the place and a red dye to put on his wounds to help dry them out so they'd close.

When we took Zeik home, we put the dye on him. It made it look like he was bleeding from everywhere. It broke my heart. We only had two options: to hold him throughout the day and night or put him on his tummy. It exhausts me now even thinking about this.

Between the steroid cream, the flare-up, and the red dye fiasco, I started searching for holistic options. I also wanted to find the source, the reason why this was happening to our baby. I asked, *What are practical things we can do to help his skin?* After research and more research, I finally found a specialist, a physician who had studied holistic medicine. She epitomized the best of both worlds, in my eyes. She portrayed herself as an eczema coach, having suffered from it for years.

She desired to help others diagnosed with eczema.

Rafe and I did a consultation call, and it brought me so much peace. *Finally! Someone to talk to who can affirm my research and help us all navigate eczema.* Having a plan for how to tackle this condition got me and Rafe on the same page.

There were changes to Zeik's diet, a supplement plan, a bath routine . . . so many things. After six months of working with this holistic doctor, Zeik's skin looked amazing. We were off the steroid cream. We continue to do everything we can for his skin. Sadly, I know not everyone can afford to work with a specialist like this, and it saddens me when I talk to other new moms who aren't knowledgeable about the simple things they can do for their children who are suffering through eczema. I'm not going to put all my tips in this book—because everyone is different, and I'm not a specialist—but I will extend an invitation to email me. If you email me needing support when it comes to eczema, I'll give you all the tips and encouragement I can and provide some resources that were helpful for us. Remember: you're not alone.

So why were we going through this? Do any of us know the answer to that question when it comes to our hardships?

I didn't know my baby was going to have these health issues. No one signs up for their struggles. I didn't know how hard it was going to be, being a mom.

And the fact that it was challenging made me feel guilty. I'm not saying I wished I didn't have Zeik (not at all), but it was hard seeing other friends with healthy babies while we were struggling.

That's when I thought of Mary, the mother of Jesus. What did she think when she saw her son being beaten, bleeding, and then hanging from a cross? Could she have thought, *I didn't sign up for this?* Maybe. But God chose her to be His mother for a godly reason, just like how God chose me to be Zeik's mom. And just like God has chosen you for your baby. Sometimes, in the moment, we might not understand why something is happening, especially if it's hard, traumatic, or stressful. But we can trust that God will use it for good. There is nothing that Jesus hasn't felt. He went through suffering and pain too. So, if you need someone to understand yours, you have a God that gets it—a God who isn't going to leave you alone in it. He will bring you hope when you feel hopeless. You can cling to Him because He's a God who will bring you rest. A God who can bring you peace as no one else can . . . and a hope unlike any you've had when everything feels like it's falling apart.

God's love got me through the loss of my grandma, having a baby in a global pandemic, loneliness, the healing of my body, and struggles with my new body. He gave me strength when I felt like I had nothing left to give, helping us through our eczema battle and blessing me with my husband and family who support me.

I know that I'm going to continue to advocate for Zeik throughout his life. I'll be a voice for him as he grows into a young man.

I think it's easy to get caught up in us doing this thing called parenthood by ourselves. We tend to forget that we also have an Advocate. For John 14:16–17 says:

And I will ask the Father, and he will give you another advocate to help you and be with you forever—the Spirit of truth. The world cannot accept him, because it neither sees him nor knows him. But you know him, for he lives with you and will be in you.

What does that mean for us? God, Jesus, and the Holy Spirit are one. The Holy Spirit is unique, as He lives within us. He's our counselor when we're in need. He's the truth that lives within our soul, even when lies from the enemy are being whispered into our ears. You know the ones—the lies that you're not a good mom, you fall short in some way, you won't get through whatever you're going through, God isn't there for you, you're alone, or you're a failure. These lies can seep in, but they're lies that hold no truth.

Jesus asked His Father to give us the Holy Spirit as One who will be with us forever, One who only bears truth. We also have the Bible to read truth, to learn where our true identity lies. We are children of God.

We have a choice every day to live in that truth. To hone our ability to feel and hear the Spirit that lives within us. We can choose to love and serve others radically. Some days are easier than others, and some days the world just gets to us, and we forget we have that Counselor who hears us, knows us, and will defend us.

But maybe, just maybe . . . you've made it this far into this book and you haven't accepted Jesus as your Lord and Savior. You haven't experienced the Holy Spirit. I hope right now you feel a warmth in your heart. A nudge, a feeling, a yearning for more. I pray that you surrender to that prompting to seek help, guidance, and a love that will never fail you. To feel known, cherished, and loved for simply being you. If you want to say yes to Jesus, it's simple. You can right now, this very moment. First, read this Scripture:

> *If you openly declare that Jesus is Lord and believe in your heart that God raised him from the dead, you will be saved. For it is by believing in your heart that you are made right with God, and it is by openly declaring your faith that you are saved. (Romans 10:9–10 NLT)*

Let's just reword this Scripture a bit to personalize it. I encourage you to speak it aloud:

> *God, I declare that Jesus is Lord with all of my heart. That You raised him from the dead.*

Bish, bash, bosh! How simple was that? If you just declared that and believe it in your heart, *I'm so excited for you!* Welcome to the family.

Or maybe you're in a season of your life where you needed to redeclare it. Maybe you needed your faith to be refreshed. Let this be a reminder that you don't have to do this thing called motherhood (or life!) all on your own. You can choose to let go of your attempt to control everything and let God in to do the heavy lifting and burden carrying. Let Him into every area of your life.

Prayer

Father and Spirit, I pray this Scripture for all to hear and accept as Your promise to us: "Peace I leave with you; my peace I give you. I do not give to you as the world gives. Do not let your hearts be troubled and do not be afraid." (John 14:27)

CHAPTER TWELVE

Momma Prayers

COVERING YOU IN PRAYER

I want to leave you filled with the power of prayer.
These are prayers from other moms I know from all
around the world. I hope they bless you, give you
strength, and remind you that you're not alone in what
you're going through. Don't isolate yourself—join or
build a community of women willing to support you.
Just know that people won't know how to support you
if you don't tell them you're in need. Please never feel
ashamed about it. We all need each other.

Praise be to the God and Father of our Lord
Jesus Christ, the Father of compassion and the

God of all comfort, who comforts us in all our
troubles, so that we can comfort those in any
trouble with the comfort we ourselves receive
from God. (2 Corinthians 1:3–4)

Jesus, we thank You for the miracle of life. I pray that no matter where in the journey of motherhood we are, You would remind us that we are not alone. That we can have joy in the journey. Sleepless nights and the weight of raising a life can be overwhelming. We ask for Your peace and comfort to flood our thoughts. Let us rest in the truth of your Word and the presence of Your Spirit. I pray for divine fellowship and community to surround this life. That Your faithfulness would be so clear to us from the early years of motherhood through adult life. Thank You for Your provision and grace. Thank You for choosing us to love and care for these children. We speak Your purpose and identity into them. We ask for strength in navigating the things of this world. Give us Your perspective and wisdom to share. Help us to always lead them back to You and Your plans for them. Thank You, Jesus, for this gift. Amen.

Sarah Parker, Oregon, USA

———

I'm praying for you as you enter this beautiful, ex-hilarating, new journey of motherhood. I pray that you would rest in the hands of the Father as you raise your new little one. I pray that in the seasons of weariness, feeling overwhelmed by all the needs and the lack of time, the long days and sometimes longer nights, the wiping of the tears, the endless rocking, the constant feedings and piles of laundry that grow at your feet—I pray for you, sweet mama, that you would know just how strong you are. I pray that you would be filled with grace and strength from our heavenly Father. I pray in the moments when you feel as though you are not enough that you would run to the arms of the Father, for He is your refuge, your very present help in time of need. He sees you, new mama, and He is ever ready to wrap His arms of strength and grace around you. There will be both beautiful days and challenging days. Days when your heart is overcome with a love you've never known possible. Days when you long to rediscover who you are apart from this new role you've now entered into. The Lord is present in both of these days. Let Him whisper gently to your soul, reviving, reminding, and renewing your spirit one day at a time. I pray for wisdom for your season of motherhood. I pray that God would guide your feet as you carry your young. May you sense the Lord illuminating your path with His peace and His light as you navigate a road unfamiliar. May you draw upon His fresh grace and mercy that awaits you with each new sunrise. Trust in His goodness, rest in His peace, draw upon His strength, seek His wisdom, and walk in confidence knowing that our Father is for you and with you, present and ready to pour out His lavish love upon your heart and soul. Amen.

Keirsten Jones, Oregon, USA

––––––

Trust in the Lord with all your heart and lean not on your own understanding; In all your ways submit to Him, and he will make your paths straight. (Proverbs 3:5–6)

May God assist you in this beautiful journey and give you all the strength you need to protect and raise your children. May He teach you the deepest love you'll ever know. May He give you endless patience for the hardest moments because His faithful love never ends.

Remember, none of us is perfect. Forgive yourself and lift it all up to Him in prayers. Ask for His forgiveness, for His help in letting go of any negative emotions or stress.

God is good, God is great! AMEN!

Maddalena Crackett, London, UK

––––––

Momma, Daughter,

God has entrusted you with the highest of honors.

He has chosen you to create, carry, and bring life into this world. God holds you in the highest regard. You are trustworthy, you are capable, and you are worthy of mothering your child. You are powerful.

It is in partnership—in oneness with Christ—that I approach the throne on your behalf. My prayer for you, Momma, is this:

Momma, I pray you know your power. Your breath is powerful. It escorts in the Holy Spirit, and it sends away darkness. It heals. Keep breathing. In moments of pain, breathe. In moments of overwhelm, breathe. I pray the breath of Heaven over you now. In Jesus's name, anxiety, leave. Momma, may you be filled with confidence in your ability to discern what your baby needs. In Jesus's name, may depression lift, and may you be filled with lightness. In Jesus's name, hormones, stabilize.

I pray resources over you, Momma. You have options. You are not stuck. In Jesus's name, we break agreement with the lies of "shoulds" and expectations. Momma, you are what your baby needs, and making choices that give you respite is okay.

Lord, thank You for Your provision. We ask for a village to surround this momma. We ask for excellent lactation consultants to be accessible, for financial provision to buy formula; we ask for neighbors to bring meals, many arms to hold the baby, and a community of women to encourage at all hours of the day and night.

Momma, I pray healing over your body. Papa, thank

You that Your body was broken for us so You know our physical pain. You understand our tears, and You, too, agonized on behalf of your children. The hymn "How Great Thou Art" says, "There on that cross, my burden gladly bearing, He bled . . ." Thank You for loving us so much that You bled and died with gladness, Jesus. I ask for that source of gladness, Jesus.

When we are afraid our lives will always look like endless cycles of feeding, exhaustion, and emotion, I pray for gladness, Lord. When we don't feel connected to our newborn—gladness, Lord. When the nipples are cracked and bleeding—more gladness, Lord, in even the most unexpected of moments. I pray for perseverance.

Thank You for believing in the greatness of women, Lord. Thank You for declaring that we are holy, trustworthy leaders and mentors and sources of wisdom and influence in this world. Thank You for creating us as life-givers, worthy co-laborers with You. Thank You for the power of mothering.

Momma, may this be a reminder of your worth today, that your identity hasn't been lost in this journey of motherhood, but rather, it's evolving. Believe that it will be something far more refining and impactful than you could have imagined. I am cheering you on. You are not alone. Amen.

Emily Hartley, Oregon, USA

———

Lord,

I pray for myself and all moms. I pray that every day, You will renew our spirits in You. That every mom will recognize the strength, patience, and perseverance You've given us in the moments we feel like we're drowning. That when it feels like we have nothing else left to give, You will sustain us. Further, I pray that in those moments, our children will see how to rely on You. Pause our racing thoughts and self-imposed time limits and give us the patience to linger in Your presence. Help us not react in frustration but breathe and take a moment to guide our children toward You in every circumstance. I pray that our tongues will profess Your goodness and that our actions will portray Your love for those around us. Thank You, God, that You are always with us and that we get to connect with You. Thank You for the example You give us to share with our children—that even when we fail (and oh, we fail constantly), Your love is unfailing and non-circumstantial. Lord, I pray that You will draw close to the mom who feels overworked, run down, far from herself, and who compares herself to other moms. I pray that in You she will be renewed—that she will find strength, perseverance, and grace for herself, and that she will see and KNOW she is THE chosen and BEST mother for her children. Amen.

Haley Dameron, Alabama, USA

Father God,

Bless this mother. In this remarkable, transforming season, abound in Your goodness to her.

Give her joy. With every discovery, may she be grateful and glad. Give her wonder, giggles, and intimacy. Help her treasure it all.

Turn this joy to strength. May she weather the storms of hormones and interrupted sleep. May she feel in her body and spirit a deepening capacity for care.

Share this strength in community. May she know she is surrounded. May she find the source of comfort and encouragement that matches who she is. Give her friends who understand.

We trust you, God. Amen.

Hannah Grayson, Edinburgh, UK

———

Dear Lord Jesus,

I come before You recognizing that no two life stories are the same, but also that loss, whatever that looks like, connects us all: pain, disappointment, unbearable heartbreak, fear, and an overwhelming feeling that immobilizes us mentally and physically. As Your daughter Caitlyn has portrayed so well in her story, You, dear God, also know my story of losing a young adult son, and the individual losses of many women reading this book. In our grief, we need You more than we know, desiring to comprehend Your purposes when we don't understand, and increasingly wanting to exchange the deepest and darkest of days with a miracle that forever changes us.

Lord Jesus, I ask that You would redeem those places of deep hurt with glimpses of overwhelming Joy. Give all of us patience when we have yet to understand and remind us of the eternal Hope of Heaven where every tear will be wiped away and the undeniable thick fog of the present will be replaced with the clarity of fine crystal. It's in this space we ask that You would replace our cries of pain with the cry of "HOLY, HOLY, HOLY is the Lord God Almighty."

Just as Mary had yet to understand the brevity of life change, both in conception and the raising and the losing of her Son, we trust Your plan to go beyond what we could even ask or imagine. For in Mary's willing-ness to lose "her plan," an entire world was given the opportunity to be saved from sin, the ultimate healing. Lord Jesus, may that sink into every fiber of our beings. If we surrender to Your purposes, a redemptive story has the opportunity to unfold, one petal at a time. As a result, not only are we changed, but we are given new wings to encourage one another to see You for who You are, Lord Jesus Christ, the Savior, Healer, and Hope for every woman, man, and child.

Thank You for the reminder You gave me in 2015 after losing my *only* son . . . "He heals the brokenhearted and binds up their wounds" (Psalm 147:3). Lord Jesus, I have held onto that truth and ask you do the same for every woman reading this book.

It's for Your glory and in Your healing power and name I pray. AMEN.

Keri Jackson*, Portland, OR, USA

*Married to an honorable and godly husband of forty-three years, mother of three beautiful daughters, three outstanding sons-in-law, and one amazing son who is with Jesus; and grandmother of soon-to-be four precious grandbabies.

———

Dear Lord,

I pray for every precious new and expecting mom who has had the opportunity to read this book to step bravely into their unique story with You.

Help them surrender their cares, concerns, fears, and inadequacies to You.

Please draw near to them in the midnight hours of feeding, changing, or physical discomfort and fill their hearts with joy and give them the energy they need.

Thank You that we can trust You to never give them more than they can bear, and that You are faithful to

Your Word, which says that You gently lead those with young. Amen.

Rhonwyn Vincent, Cape Town, South Africa

———

A prayer from the heart to a new mom:

Lord Jesus, let this new mom know how beautiful, strong, and ready she is for motherhood. Give her constant glimpses of the width and depth of Your love as she steps into this new season. Surround her with Your peace and supernatural power to be energized in her body. Lord, protect her from negative thoughts. Let her not focus on the changes in her body but on the miracle that has come through her body. Remind her that she is gifted and equipped for every task at hand. I declare that in Your name, nothing will steal her joy and that she will bathe in the confidence of knowing that all things will happen in Your perfect timing.

Rest in Jesus's name, Amen.

Nicole Nassar, London, UK

———

"I pray that God, the source of hope, will fill you completely with joy and peace because you trust in Him." Romans 15:13

Jesus, I first want to thank you for the gift of new life and the beauty You have in store in the coming days for each mom reading this beautiful story you have unfolded for Cait and her new family. Redeem us in this new life you have created. I pray that You would sustain us in this season and in the next. I pray that we won't lose ourselves in motherhood, rather find ourselves in it. Keep our hearts dreaming and passionate, but allow us the time to slow when You ask us too. To take in each fleeting week, month or year of motherhood we are in and really be there for our precious children. Jesus, help us in the changing seasons of motherhood. Guide our hearts and fill us with your joy and peace. Bring us community in these seasons and help us to be moms that build each other up and be examples for our children.

Lord, you are our source of every good thing. Thank you for providing for Caitlyn throughout her journey of motherhood. Help us to remember the scripture: "He never lets us down and He promises to give us everything we need." - Philippians 4:19. Amen.

Diana Bigby, Oregon, USA

––––––

My heart is not proud, Lord,
my eyes are not haughty;
I do not concern myself with great matters

or things too wonderful for me.
But I have calmed and quieted myself,
I am like a weaned child with its mother;
like a weaned child I am content.
Israel, put your hope in the Lord
both now and forevermore. (Psalm 131)

Pregnancy has its supreme highs and its deep lows, and my prayer is for all those who will read this honest and insightful book, that you will be able to cultivate a quiet heart through all the highs and lows of your pregnancy. Like a baby content in its mother's arms, may your heart know that same deep peace and contentment—that of a weaned child. Amen.

Jean Ross Russell, Notting Hill, UK

————

Dear Lord,

Thank You for this powerful mother who has carried this blessing of a child while they grew inside, protected by Your gentle and kind heart. I want to thank You for this mama and pray for protection over her during what may be a scary, unknown time, charging full force into motherhood. I pray You give peace, patience, and love during each moment. Give her the grace she needs during this period of growth and learning. Remind her she doesn't need to have it all down or be perfect in the process. Remind her to lean on You through it all and to seek help when she is in need. Give her a voice to advocate for her baby and the discernment to choose the right things for them. I pray this mama knows the unconditional love You have for her as she does for her baby. Thank you for this little miracle. Amen.

Nicole Womack, Oregon, USA

———

Lord Jesus,

I pray for this new mum. We thank You for her body and this baby that has grown inside of her. We thank You for the beautiful struggle and strength that have led to this moment of her holding her child. I pray that she will be sheltered under Your wings and wrapped up in community. I pray that she will be able to face the challenge of this transition to a new life with grace while being present to the enormity of this miracle and the beauty that has come to her life. I pray that You keep her safe, that she will feel safe, loved, and wrapped up in Your love during this extraordinary season. I pray for time and space to look after her heart and her body. I pray that she will be able to embrace motherhood and everything that comes with it. I pray that any insecurities about her body will be completely overshadowed by awe for the strength that her body has shown. I pray that whatever feelings she has toward her birth, she will have time and emotional capacity to process them. Jesus, I pray that she will not be lonely or feel alone in times of being awake in the early hours of the morning nor overwhelmed by another life and another being's needs. I pray for wonder to outshine challenges, I pray for community over abandonment, and I pray for strength in moments of overwhelm and abundance of provision when resources seem tight. Most of all, I pray for strength, peace, and confidence. Amen.

Sophia van Deventer, London, UK

————

To be.

In the stillness of this empty room, I hold to the miracle of you.

For now, the world and life, in all of its hurry and complications, cease, because I belong to the freshness and Glory that God has knit into you.

We have been together, you and I, since your creation and conception, but now as you have been unveiled to me I sit and stare. I ponder where your life will take you, what is to become. What it means to be your mother, what stories I will tell of you, what you will teach me in this life.

At this moment, all I long for is to be with you. To study you, soak in each whimper and sigh. I trace your fragile skin with my fingertip, knowing that these fleeting moments together will forever be ingrained in my mother's heart. You are my precious gift, and I cannot unsee you as my baby no matter the size you will become.

You, my baby, are the hope for tomorrow, the promise of new beginnings that even life through the shadows will see better days. You will go beyond me in this life and all I can do is to soak in these moments and just be. Be still. Be present. Be content. Be grateful. Be peaceful. Be thankful. Be loved. This time, these moments, all I want is to just be. To behold you. The world may be waiting, but I will continue to hold on to each of your precious soft, breaths and just be.

Prayer:

May our generous and giving God create a space of peace over you and your precious babe. May the fullness and richness of His goodness and compassion be ever-present as you face each challenge. We ask, Father, for Your guidance for Your daughter. May she feel treasured, assured, and made whole in Your presence. Guide her heart toward Your mercies that are fresh each morning, and let her stand strong in your abiding and unceasing love.

Allie Montgomery, Oregon, USA

———

Dear God,

Help us bring these little souls closer to You in every way that we can. We will mess up and make the wrong decisions, but let their hearts be anchored in You. Give us grace for ourselves as we travel these unknown roads. Help us cast our anxiety on You daily so that we may be present in these fleeting moments.

Thank You for this gift of motherhood; may we make You proud of how we raise them. Amen,

Jenn Spinnet, Oregon, USA

———

Father,

I come before You to lift this mommy up to You in prayer. You see her fears, insecurities, and weaknesses and know every thought of her heart.

I pray that You would come as her heavenly Father and wrap her in your arms. Surround her with your Holy Spirit's presence. We know that in her weakness she will be made strong in You. You will give her all the wisdom and discernment she needs to raise this baby as a child of the King.

I pray You would give her the confidence each day that she is doing her very best. We speak against any comparisons that would come into her thoughts, saying that she does not measure up. You have chosen her as the perfect mother for this baby and entrusted her with their care to fulfill the divine purpose of their life. You have given her all that she needs to accomplish this.

I believe that through her love for this child, she will experience and know, without a doubt, the immeasurable fullness of Your love for her. I pray that her relationship with You would be strengthened every day as she calls on your name, Jesus.

Fill her heart with joy for the journey.

In Jesus's name, Amen.

"For I am the Lord your God who takes hold of your right hand and says to you, 'Do not fear; I will help you.'" (Isaiah 41:13)
"For when I am weak, then I am strong." (2 Corinthians 12:10 NKJV)
"Let all that you do be done with love." (I Corinthians 16:14 NKJV)
". . . the joy of the Lord is your strength." (Nehemiah 8:10 NKJV)

Lynette Malmin, Oregon, USA

———

Dear Lord,

I praise You and thank You for the story You have unfolded for Caitlyn. Thank You for the opportunity she now has to bless others by sharing her experience of walking through hard times and coming out the other side stronger and closer to You. I pray that these beautiful words are able to reach the depths of every woman's heart reading her story. Thank You for giving us hearts of courage and strength. I pray this book is the beginning of a great chapter for Caitlyn and her family. I ask that You bless the journey for this book and the audience it will reach. We lift all of this to You, in Jesus's name. Amen.

Alysha Ahrens, Oregon, USA

––––––––

Pregnancy, birth, and postpartum are never what we anticipate, good or bad. In the midst of so much joy, our bodies changing, hormones fluctuating, and minimal sleep, we are meant to be supported. When people say "it takes a village," they aren't kidding!

My prayer is that countless women will resonate with Caitlyn's story of experiencing pregnancy, birth, and postpartum (all while being faced with some of life's hardest challenges).

I pray that after reading Caitlyn's story, women who are walking through pregnancy more alone than they imagined will feel the comfort and peace that only God brings. I pray that women who are about to give birth will feel their burden lifted off their shoulders as they read through Caitlyn's story. Lastly, I pray that as women read Caitlyn's story and are walking through postpartum, they will experience healing over their bodies, minds, and spirits.

Thank You, God, for the story that Caitlyn has to share. Thank you for the hardships and joys that she experienced, not knowing that the struggles she faced and the joy she beheld were meant to be a story that could someday help so many other women.

Bethany Small, Washington, USA

———

Closing Prayer

Lord, I thank You for all the women in this chapter. Women who have walked alongside me in motherhood. Women who have gone before me and shared their wisdom with me. I pray for every woman who is reading these prayers. That they feel showered and covered with love. May they deeply know these prayers are for them. I hope they know that even if they feel alone that they are not. That there is a community of mothers that are also experiencing the joys and trials of motherhood. I pray You give them the strength to reach out when they're in need. The joy to celebrate little victories with those around them. I pray that they never feel shame of a negative thought that passes by. Or feel as if they have failed or fallen short. Protect their minds and hearts. Remind them that they can always lean on You for comfort. I hope they have a deep sense of knowing that they are seen and loved. That they are first Your daughter before becoming a mother. That their identity lies in You alone. I'm so grateful for how You are shaping us in this new season and teaching us more about who You are and Your love for your children. May You give us peace that surpasses all understanding. (Philippians 4:7) Amen.

Cait MacDonell

Shalom

CPSIA information can be obtained
at www.ICGtesting.com
Printed in the USA
JSHW080229261122
33757JS00003B/85